Department of the Environment

Sarah Fielder &
Robert Smith

London: HMSO

ISBN 011 753 2142

B2311 01/96 DDP Services

Acknowledgements

The research was commissioned by the Department of the Environment and was carried out partly within the Department's Building Stock Research Division, using data from the English House Condition Survey, and partly by researchers at the Centre for Housing Management and Development, University of Wales, Cardiff, and by MORI.

Although this is a joint publication, the research contractor, CHMD, University of Wales, Cardiff, is responsible for the recommendations. They do not necessarily reflect the views of the Department.

The authors would like to thank members of the research Steering Group for their guidance throughout the project, as well as those who participated in the research itself, particularly the case study local authorities. The significant contribution of staff at CHMD, University of Wales, in carrying out the case studies and providing secretarial support, and at MORI, in undertaking the survey of owners of vacant (and previously vacant) property, is also acknowledged.

Contents

Executive Summary

Background

It is inevitable that there will be a number of dwellings vacant at any given time to allow the housing system to function effectively, facilitating both residential mobility and the improvement or redevelopment of the stock. Different data sources give a vacancy rate in the total housing stock of between 3.4% and 4.6% in 1991. However, vacancy rates are greater in the private sector than in either local authority or housing association owned stock. There has been little research on the nature and extent of the problem and how this has changed over time. In the private sector little is known about the reasons why housing becomes and remains empty, and how and why it is brought back into use.

The Research

The aim of this research was to define the vacant private housing stock and establish how this has changed over time, in order to determine the scope for reducing the numbers of vacant dwellings by bringing more of them back into use. Specifically, the objectives of the research were:

- to identify the scale and distribution of private sector vacancies in relation to the total housing stock;
- to establish changes in the nature and extent of vacant dwellings over time;
- to determine different types of vacancy in the private sector;
- to categorise the flow of vacant dwellings; their origins (generation), duration, prolongation and termination, and changes over time;
- to define and assess the existence of a core of long term vacancies;
- to establish the prime reasons for vacancy generation, prolongation and termination and specifically the contributions made by stock condition and the nature of the housing market;
- to identify changes in legislation, strategy and policy which might facilitate bringing vacant dwellings back into use;
- to identify best practices in local authorities designed to bring empty private housing back into use and consider their wider applicability.

Part one, carried out by the Department, analysed data from the 1986 and 1991 English House Condition Surveys (EHCS), in order to identify different types of vacancy in the private sector and change over time.

In *part two*, dwellings identified as vacant in either the 1986 or 1991 EHCS (and in a few cases both years) were followed up and the owners responsible for bringing the dwellings back into use (and a small number of owners of still vacant housing) were traced and interviewed in 1994. This part sought to explain how and why private sector housing became vacant, stayed vacant and was brought back into use. From a sample of 807 addresses, interviews were conducted with 265 owners.

In *part three,* six local authority case studies were undertaken to examine strategies, policies and practices used at a local level to bring private empty dwellings back into use, and to examine the costs and outcomes of particular policy options.

Nature and Scale of Vacancy

Analysis of EHCS data has shown that, whilst the vast majority of the private sector housing stock was occupied at the time of both the 1986 and 1991 surveys, only 60% had the same residents in both years, and a third was occupied but changed residents between the two surveys. A high proportion may have been vacant at some point between the surveys, as well as those actually identified as vacant at the time of the EHCS. Mobility of residents and turnover of housing stock is higher in the private rented sector than amongst owner occupiers and is more likely to involve a period of vacancy. Thus vacancy is a necessary phenomenon to allow the housing market to function.

Rather than examining a total number of private sector vacants, the EHCS analysis has distinguished two types of private sector vacancies. ***Transactional*** vacants are active in the market and might be expected to be re-occupied relatively quickly; they are necessary for mobility in the housing market. ***Problematic*** vacants are often in poor condition and vacancy is likely to be prolonged. It is problematic vacants which may require policy action in order to bring them back into use more quickly. At any one time there are about 250,000 problematic vacants in the private sector.

Problematic vacancies are over-represented amongst the private-rented sector. They tend to be concentrated amongst pre 1919 terraced houses and converted flats and are more likely to be in poor condition compared with transactional vacants. Urban areas have more than their fair share of problematic vacants, as do the North West and Inner London.

Half of problematic vacancies would cost more than £5,000 to bring back into long term use. Renovation and modernisation have an important role to play in bringing problematic vacants back into use. Although problematic vacants had an average market value significantly lower than similar occupied dwellings, they had an aggregate value of over £13 billion in 1991, indicating that vacant housing also represents a financial waste.

Vacancy Processes

In a follow-up survey of owners of vacants, in 1994, most had undergone a change in ownership before being brought back into use. Only one fifth of owners responsible for bringing dwellings back into use were also responsible for generating the original vacancy. Landlords, however, were more likely to be responsible for both generating and ending the vacancy, although with most landlords the vacancy was generated as a result of the actions of tenants rather than the owners. This confirms the EHCS evidence that mobility (and rate of vacancy generation) is greater in the private rented sector than amongst owner occupied housing.

However, a change of occupancy in the private rented sector may not involve a change of ownership.

The main reason for vacancy generation was related to the death of the previous occupant or their movement into hospital or long term care (27% and 14% respectively giving a total of 41%). Other reasons included repossession or eviction (13%), or the former residents simply moved out for other reasons. The reasons vacancies were generated were similar whether they were subsequently classed as problematic or transactional. However, the proportion of previously owner occupied vacants which had been repossessed was higher amongst problematic vacants.

There was a wide variation in the duration of vacancy. In particular, problematic vacants and those previously privately rented typically remained empty for longer periods than other types of vacancy.

Two distinct periods of vacancy can be identified: firstly when the vacancy is generated, and, secondly, where there is a change of ownership, there is sometimes a period of vacancy after acquisition. Reasons for the vacancy being prolonged after generation were primarily concerned with the poor condition of the dwelling, or difficulties experienced in selling or letting the vacant dwelling, or complications over ownership. After acquisition, the dwelling may not be occupied immediately and this was overwhelmingly related to repairs and renovations which had to be undertaken. A lack of resources for improvement was often a major barrier to the speedy re-use of empty housing. However, in other cases prolonging vacancy is a prelude to the loss of the dwelling from the housing stock, through change of use or demolition.

Bringing Vacants Back into Use

Where vacant dwellings have been brought back into use by owner occupiers, they are predominantly small adult households which are economically active, and at a relatively early stage in their housing career. Because of their relatively low market value and concentration in the older housing stock, vacant dwellings provide opportunities for such households to enter owner occupation. Nearly two thirds of such households were in skilled manual occupations, some with the relevant skills to renovate property which was in poor condition.

Organisations acquiring vacant dwellings are diverse. Some have acquired dwellings with the primary intention of letting them to tenants, others have acquired vacant residential property as part of a commercial package and may let the property to tenants, or use the accommodation to house employees. However, in some instances the acquisition of vacant residential space has been by default, with the owners having no real interest in either occupying or letting the premises.

The factors determining acquisition for residential use included the location of the property, the opportunity to renovate, and most significantly, that the price was affordable and represented good value. Prices paid for vacant dwellings were generally low, particularly amongst those classified as problematic and those acquired by private landlords. The relatively low price of vacancies may reflect their original condition (and subsequent deterioration during vacancy), and the willingness of vendors to reduce the selling price the longer a property remains vacant. Whilst the low price of problematic vacancies may enable those on relatively low incomes to become owner occupiers, perhaps for the first time, the condition of the property may delay re-occupation whilst the necessary renovations are financed and carried out.

Local Authority Action

The local authority case studies confirmed that there are limited accurate sources of data on the scale of vacants at the local level, and that current methods of estimating private sector vacants vary between local authorities. A consistent source is needed. With appropriate staffing resources a local register of problematic vacancies could be developed. These properties could be monitored, the owners traced and action taken to encourage either their re-use or their acquisition for clearance.

Empty property strategies may be driven by different motives, for example meeting housing need, or tackling problems of urban renewal, or perhaps a combination. They use a variety of policy initiatives, many of which are aimed at the private rented sector. It may be more appropriate to target leasing and management schemes towards the owners of empty dwellings which are self-contained and in reasonably good condition, if the priority is to maximise the number of additional units brought back into use for those in housing need. Alternatively, grant aided initiatives, perhaps linked to leasing or management schemes, may be more urgent if the priority is to bring back into use some of the empty dwellings in the most serious disrepair.

The evidence from the case studies suggests that, in terms of numbers of dwellings, policy initiatives have collectively had only a limited impact upon vacancies, and action is highly resource intensive. However, even on a relatively small scale, they contribute to the re-use of previously empty housing. They make an impact at the local level, and may also have a knock on effect, in encouraging other owners to return empty dwellings into use more quickly than they otherwise might.

Policy Issues

Vacancy should not only be seen as a waste of a valuable asset and a lost housing opportunity. Vacancy in the private sector also allows the housing system to function, by facilitating mobility and renovation. However, some vacants do present a problem. Local authorities need to develop efficient systems and procedures for monitoring empty private housing, particularly problematic vacants. Only by developing mechanisms to collect information on which properties are vacant, how long they have been vacant, and why they remain vacant, will it be possible to target the most problematic vacancies and devise appropriate schemes to ensure their re-use.

Up to date guidance is needed on measures available to local authorities to tackle private sector empty housing, and in what circumstances individual measures, or a combination, should be used, since there is a diversity of options available with different funding sources. Most action is aimed at the private rented sector, but different solutions are appropriate according to the circumstances of vacancy and ownership.

In addition to the initiatives already available to local authorities, other mechanisms which might be considered are:

- tax incentives for private landlords to encourage them to undertake repairs and improvements of vacant property;
- funding for housing association rehabilitation of CPO acquired empty properties;
- strengthening powers available to local authorities where an owner is deliberately withholding a property from the market.

1 Setting the Scene

Background

1.1 Empty housing is the most visible form of stock under-utilisation. Social landlords are now performing relatively well in reducing and controlling the level of vacancy within their own stock, but the private sector has a significantly higher vacancy rate. Yet knowledge of vacancy in the private sector is limited. Since privately owned housing may become and remain empty for different reasons from socially owned housing, different policies and action may be needed to bring them back into use.

1.2 Information on the scale, ownership and location of vacant housing is available from various sources.[1] Three sources of data for 1991 are available at a national level: the Census of Population, the English House Condition Survey (EHCS) and Housing Strategy and Investment Programme (HIP) returns made by local authorities. Since each set of information is compiled in a very different way, it is unsurprising that they give very different estimates of the scale of vacancy (Table 1.1).

1.3 The differences in vacancy rate may be explained by the fact that these estimates were made at different times during the year, using different definitions and methodologies. However, adjusting for definitional variation, it is estimated that total vacancies in 1991 ranged between 655,000 and 888,000, giving an overall vacancy rate of between 3.4% and 4.6%.

Table 1.1 Comparison of Different Estimates of the Number of Vacant Dwellings, England 1991

Ownership	Census No.	EHCS No.	HIP No.
Private Sector	N/A[1]	508,000[2]	638,000
Housing Associations	N/A	18,000	15,000
Central Government/ other public sector	N/A	N/A	14,000
Local Authority/New Town	N/A	113,000	81,000
Total	**905,000**	**639,000**	**749,000**

Notes: 1 Not Available
2 EHCS figures include dwellings owned by central government as these were classed as 'other private landlord'.

1.4 At the local level a number of studies have focused on the issue of privately owned empty housing (including Shelter (Scotland), 1985; Williams, 1987; Prosser, 1992). These have often been action research projects designed not only to identify private sector empty dwellings and the reasons for vacancy, but also to bring as many as possible back into use. In addition, a DoE study of vacant private sector dwellings in five local authority areas in 1987/88 (Finch, Lovell and Ward, 1989)

1 for a review of sources of information on vacancies, see Smith and Merrett, 1987.

provided qualitative information on why dwellings in private ownership became empty and remained empty.

1.5 Guidance on Housing Strategies (1995) from DoE now urges local authorities to adopt empty housing strategies, whilst £30 million of Housing Partnership funds have been made available in 1995/96 to support housing projects, with particular emphasis given to schemes which bring empty dwellings back into use.

1.6 Most studies have analysed private sector vacancies at one point in time. But these vacancies are the product of two processes which occur through time: the rate at which vacancies are generated and the average length of time these dwellings remain empty. Therefore a high absolute number of empty dwellings is not a problem in itself, and it should not be assumed that such a stock is permanently wasted. Housing choice and mobility can only be exercised by households where there is a flow of vacancies.

1.7 To understand the processes which result in vacant dwellings, a longitudinal analysis is required. This can be achieved by using data on vacancies from the Department's 1986 and 1991 English House Condition Surveys (EHCS). These data can be used to gain a clearer picture of the characteristics of vacant dwellings in the private sector, and how they changed from one survey to the next. In addition, by tracing the owners of these dwellings, this study seeks to understand the reasons dwellings become and remain vacant, and how they are brought back into use.

Research Objectives

1.8 Some level of vacancy is essential if the housing system is to function efficiently, facilitating both mobility and renewal. But it is not known what proportion of the stock needs to be vacant for this purpose and why dwellings become and remain vacant. The aim of the research was to define the vacant private housing stock, establish how this has changed over time, achieve a better understanding of movement into and out of vacancy and consider how private sector vacancies might be brought back into use. Specifically, the objectives of the study were:

- to identify the scale and distribution of private sector vacancies in relation to the total housing stock;
- to establish changes in the nature and extent of vacant dwellings over time;
- to determine different types of vacancy in the private sector;
- to categorise the flow of vacant dwellings, their generation, duration, prolongation and termination, and changes over time;
- to define and assess the existence of a core of long term vacancies;
- to establish the prime reasons for vacancy generation, prolongation and termination, particularly in respect of long term vacancies and specifically the contributions made by stock condition and the nature of the housing market;

- to identify changes in legislation, strategy and policy which might facilitate the re-use of private sector vacancies;
- to identify best practices in local authorities designed to bring empty housing back into use and consider their wider applicability.

Defining Vacancy

1.9 The study includes residential property owned prior to vacancy by individuals or private sector organisations and excludes property owned prior to vacancy by housing associations and local authorities.

1.10 This study uses dwellings rather than household spaces as the unit of analysis, as dwellings are the basis of the EHCS. EHCS surveyors were instructed to categorise vacancies as awaiting sale, awaiting demolition or being modernised, or, if there was no apparent reason for vacancy, as newly vacant (within the last month), vacant medium term or vacant long term (more than six months). This categorisation relied upon a degree of interpretation, based upon visible clues and neighbours as a source of information.

1.11 However, in seeking to define vacancy, a number of questions arise over the boundaries between vacant and unoccupied property. Second homes, holiday accommodation and dwellings whose usual occupants are absent are explicitly excluded from this research, since there is a clear distinction between housing which is used for at least part of the time and where the owner has clear intentions as to its use, and housing which is not used at all.

Research Methods

1.12 The research was carried out in three parts:

- *Part One*: An analysis of the extent and characteristics of private sector vacant dwellings and how these changed, using data from the 1986 and 1991 EHCS was carried out by the Department. This was designed to develop a typology of vacancy;
- *Part Two*: A follow up survey of a sample of dwellings identified as vacant in 1986 or 1991 to identify those owners responsible for bringing the empty dwellings back into use or the owners of still vacant dwellings, and to develop an understanding of the processes by which these vacancies originated, how and why they were prolonged and how and why they were brought back into use. This was carried out by University of Wales, Cardiff, and MORI;
- *Part Three*: Case study research into the role of local authorities in stimulating the re-use of vacant dwellings in the private sector, by University of Wales, Cardiff.

1.13 Since the research was mainly concerned with establishing the reasons for private dwellings becoming empty and staying vacant, and the processes and problems in bringing vacant dwellings back into use, it has focused particularly on long term vacants. The longitudinal nature of the EHCS has provided a cohort of vacancies identified as empty either in 1986 or 1991 (or in a few cases both). Fieldwork undertaken in 1994 identified, traced and interviewed the owners of dwellings in this sample, who had brought the property back into use or have kept it vacant. Further details of the research methodology are set out in Appendix A.

Structure of Report

1.14 In chapter two the longitudinal data from the EHCS is used to examine the changing nature of private sector vacant dwellings between 1986 and 1991 and to identify different types of private sector vacants.

1.15 Chapter three discusses the results from the follow up study of vacancies to look at the processes of vacancy origin, duration and prolongation. In particular it considers why private sector housing is empty, how long such properties stay empty and why vacancy is prolonged.

1.16 Chapter four looks at how vacancies were brought back into use and why others remain vacant. It examines the processes and costs of bringing empty housing back into use and the characteristics of those owners responsible for ending the vacancy process.

1.17 Chapter five examines local authority approaches to the problem of private sector vacancy and the policy initiatives at their disposal. Finally, the report draws conclusions, examines key policy issues and offers recommendations for action by both local authorities and central government policy makers. These policy issues and recommendations were identified by University of Wales, Cardiff.

2 The Changing Nature of Private Sector Vacant Dwellings

Introduction

2.1 An analysis of English House Condition Survey data examined the extent and characteristics of vacant dwellings and how these changed between 1986 and 1991. This has enabled the identification of two main types of vacancy: 'transactional' vacants, which were active in the housing market and likely to be brought back into use quite quickly, and those vacancies which were more 'problematic'.

2.2 The total private sector stock in 1991 was over 15 million dwellings. This consisted of owner occupied, occupied private rented and vacant privately owned housing. Table 2.1 shows that the vast majority of the private sector stock (94%) was occupied at the time of both the 1986 and 1991 EHCS.

Table 2.1 Change in Private Sector Stock 1986 and 1991

	No.(000s) dwellings	**%**
Occupied 1986 and 1991	14,144	93.6
Same residents, 1986-1991	*9,115*	*60.3*
Change of residents, 1986-1991	*5,029*	*33.3*
Vacant 1986, occupied 1991	472	3.1
Vacant 1991, occupied 1986	392	2.6
Vacant 1986 and 1991	79	0.5
Newly built/converted since 1986, vacant in 1991	30	0.2
Total	**15,117**	**100.0**

2.3 Most housing had the same residents in 1986 and 1991, although a third was occupied in both years but had changed residents between the two surveys and in the process may have undergone a period of vacancy. This pattern varied considerably by tenure with a much higher level of mobility within the private rented sector stock. While 65% of the owner occupied stock was occupied by the same residents over the survey period, the same was true for less than 40% of dwellings in the private rented sector.

Identifying Problematic Vacants

2.4 Two types of vacancy were distinguished from EHCS data:

- *'transactional'* vacancies under normal market conditions might be expected to experience a relatively short period of vacancy before being bought or re-let;
- *'problematic'* vacancies are less likely to be brought back into use through the normal operation of the market and stayed vacant for some time[2].

It is this latter group which should be the focus of policy designed to bring unnecessarily vacant dwellings back into use.

2.5 The proportion of vacants classed as transactional was different in each year. In 1986, 40% of vacancies were categorised as transactional and 60% as problematic, with the respective proportions being 46% and 54% in 1991. However, vacants in the problematic category included those awaiting demolition or undergoing renovation, and these were lower in 1991 (12% of all vacants) than in 1986 (20%). The likely scale of problematic vacants at any one time, excluding demolitions and those undergoing renovation (that is, where something was being done) was estimated to be about 250,000 dwellings. The relationship between transactional and problematic vacancy is likely to change as market conditions change, with a lower proportion of problematic vacants as it becomes easier to sell empty housing, particularly to intending owner occupiers, or the effective demand for rented housing is increased, or the rate at which vacant housing is improved is accelerated.

Occupancy and Tenure Change: 1986 and 1991

2.6 Whereas 95% of the owner occupied stock in 1986 was still owner occupied in 1991, Table 2.2 shows there was a much higher movement into and out of the private rented sector, indicating a higher likelihood of vacancy amongst this sector. Whilst a majority of vacant dwellings came from or went into owner occupation, about 20% in each year either originated in the private rented sector or were brought back into use through private renting. This is higher than the proportion of the private sector as a whole which was privately rented. The private rented sector is therefore disproportionately represented amongst private sector vacants.

---

[2] The following criteria were used to classify EHCS vacants as either transactional or problematic.

(i) Transactional vacancies in 1986 were defined as either awaiting sale or short-term vacant, in good condition at that time and/or reoccupied quickly (ie length of residence of 1991 occupiers was 5 years). The remainder of those vacant in 1986 were categorised as problematic.

(ii) Transactional vacancies in 1991 were again those classed as awaiting sale or newly vacant. However, there was no information as to whether these vacants subsequently became problematic. It was assumed that any newly vacant or vacant awaiting sale dwelling identified as empty in 1991 and in poor condition was likely to be problematic. Only those in good condition of the newly vacants/awaiting sale were taken as transactional.

(iii) All those vacant in both 1986 and 1991 were classed as problematic vacancies. It is highly likely that the majority of these would have been empty over the whole five year period. Those which were not (and they are extremely difficult to identify) may still be considered problematic in that they are likely to have moved into and out of vacancy several times during this period.

Table 2.2 Origin of the 1991 Private Sector Stock (thousand dwellings)

	1991 Private Sector Stock						
	Owner occupied		Private Rented Sector		Private Sector Vacant		Total
1986 Origin	000s	%	000s	%	000s	%	000s
Owner occupied in 1986 (row %)	10,922 (94.5)	84.1	352 (3.0)	21.6	280 (2.4)	55.9	11,554 (100)
Private rented sector in 1986 (row %)	276 (19.9)	2.1	1,010 (72.8)	62.1	102 (7.3)	20.3	1,388 (100)
Local authority in 1986 (row %)	509 (89.3)	3.9	51 (8.9)	3.1	10 (1.7)	2.0	570 (100)
Vacant in 1986 (row %)	417 (64.8)	3.2	147 (22.9)	9.0	79 (12.3)	15.8	643 (100)
Newly built/ Converted since 1986 (row %)	866 (90.0)	6.7	66 (6.9)	4.1	30 (3.1)	6.0	962 (100)
Total	**12,990**	**(100)**	**1,626**	**(100)**	**501**	**(100)**	**15,117**

2.7 In addition, Table 2.3 shows that former private rented dwellings accounted for a higher proportion of problematic vacants (27%) than they did of transactional vacants (17%). However, the problematic total includes those dwellings vacant in both 1986 and 1991 for which tenure cannot be allocated. Thus, the proportion of problematic private rented vacancies is likely to be even higher than shown. If the emphasis of policy is towards tackling problematic vacants, which may have been vacant for relatively long intervals, then it is likely that attention will need to be focused on vacancies owned by private landlords.

Table 2.3 Tenure of Vacant Dwellings (1986 or 1991) by Vacancy Type

	Vacancy Type			
	Problematic		Transactional	
Tenure (Origin or Destination)	No. (000s)	%	No. (000s)	%
Owner occupied in 1986 or 1991	229	57.4	336	74.3
Private rented in 1986 or 1991	141	27.1	77	17.0
Local authority in 1986, private sector vacant in 1991	1	0.2	9	2.0
Vacant in 1986 and 1991	79	15.2	-	-
New or converted since 1986, vacant in 1991	-	-	30	6.6
Total	**521**	**(100.0)**	**452**	**(100.0)**

The Characteristics of Private Sector Vacant Dwellings

Age and Type of Dwelling

2.8 Over two thirds of problematic vacancies (identified in 1986 or 1991) were built before 1919, compared with less than a third of the occupied private stock in 1991 (Table 2.4). They were much more likely to be terraced houses (43.2%) or converted flats (15.6%), whilst detached and semi-detached houses were under-represented amongst problematic vacants. Transactional vacancies were more like the occupied stock, although the oldest (pre-1919) stock was still over-represented. This probably reflects the fact that older housing provides for a significant

Table 2.4 Age and Property Type of Problematic Vacant Dwellings

Age/Dwelling Type	Occupied Private Stock 1991 No.(000s)	Occupied Private Stock 1991 %	Problematic Vacants No. (000s)	Problematic Vacants %
Pre 1919	4,234	29.9	358	68.7
1919-1944	2,805	19.8	81	15.5
1945-1964	2,461	17.4	40	7.7
Post 1964	4,661	32.9	42	8.1
Terraced house	3,736	26.4	225	43.2
Semi-detached	4,172	29.5	101	19.4
Detached	2,791	19.7	57	10.9
Bungalow	1,400	9.9	20	3.8
Converted flat	1,205	8.5	81	15.6
Purpose-built flat	857	6.0	37	7.1
Total	**14,161**	**(100.0)**	**521**	**(100.0)**

Table 2.5 Location of Problematic Vacants by Region

Region	Occupied Private Stock 1991 No. (000s)	Occupied Private Stock 1991 %	Problematic Vacants No. (000s)	Problematic Vacants %
Northern	836	5.9	22	4.2
Yorks and Humberside	1,368	9.7	54	10.4
North West	1,796	12.7	82	15.8
East Midlands	1,178	8.3	44	8.5
West Midlands	1,468	10.4	66	12.6
South West	1,556	11.0	61	11.7
East Anglia	616	4.3	24	4.5
Inner London	556	3.9	40	7.7
Outer London	1,393	9.8	40	7.6
Rest of South East	3,394	24.0	88	16.9
Total	**14,161**	**(100.0)**	**521**	**(100.0)**

proportion of the first time buyer market which is likely to have higher turnover rates.

Location

2.9 There are significant regional differences in the distribution of problematic vacancies (Table 2.5). The North West has a higher level of problematic vacancy compared to its share of the occupied stock, whilst London has a higher incidence of transactional vacants than would be expected from its share of the occupied stock. As a proportion of its private sector stock, Inner London has both the highest problematic vacancy rate and the highest transactional vacancy rate, compared to all other regions. In addition, problematic vacancies are a little more likely than transactional vacancies to be found in urban areas.

Condition

2.10 Since most problematic private sector vacancies are pre-1919 terraced houses and converted flats, the occupied stock of pre-1919 terraced houses and converted flats has been taken as a 'control' group to compare problematic vacants with other similar housing in the occupied private sector. If problematic vacancies do tend to have different characteristics from other similar occupied private housing, then it may be possible to identify those private dwellings which are more likely to become problematic vacants.

2.11 Whereas 12.6% of the control group were unfit in 1991, almost double that proportion (24.6%) of problematic vacants were unfit at that time. However, there is a considerable degree of variation amongst problematic vacants. Table 2.6 shows that those occupied in 1991, but vacant in 1986, were in better condition than those vacant in 1991. As well as indicating that problematic vacants are much more likely to be unfit than similar occupied stock, this breakdown shows that dwellings with a history of vacancy, even though occupied in 1991, were more likely to be unfit than a similar type of dwelling without such an apparent history.

2.12 Table 2.7 shows that problematic vacants in 1991 which were formerly privately rented were more likely to be unfit (42.4%) than those which had been owner occupied (32.8%). However, the situation was reversed when looking at those which were vacant in 1986 but by 1991 were re-occupied. It appears that the private rented sector was in better condition following a period of vacancy than was the owner occupied sector.

Table 2.6 Problematic vacants and control group: Rate of Unfitness

	% unfit
Occupied in 1986, but vacant in 1991	36.3%
Vacant in both 1986 and 1991	44.1%
Vacant in 1986, but occupied in 1991	16.5%
Occupied 1986 and 1991 (control group)	12.6%

Table 2.7 Problematic Vacants: Unfitness by Origin or Destination Tenure

	Fit		Unfit		Total	
Origin or Destination Tenure	**No. (000s)**	**Row %**	**No. (000s)**	**Row %**	**No. (000s)**	**Row %**
Owner occupied						
Occupied 1986, vacant 1991	84	67.2	41	32.8	125	100.0
Vacant 1986, occupied 1991	141	81.1	33	18.9	174	100.0
Total	**225**	**75.3**	**74**	**24.7**	**299**	**100.0**
Private Rented						
Occupied 1986, vacant 1991	36	57.6	26	42.4	62	100.0
Vacant 1986, occupied 1991	69	87.4	10	12.6	79	100.0
Total	**105**	**74.5**	**36**	**25.5**	**141**	**100.0**

2.14 Over half of the occupied control group showed an improvement in condition[3] over the period 1986 to 1991 (Table 2.8), whether they were owner occupied (53.1%) or privately rented (55.7%). The control group also showed some deterioration, which was higher amongst those which were privately rented (26.5%), compared with those in the owner occupied stock (20.3%).

2.15 However, the majority of those vacant in 1991, but previously occupied in 1986, had either deteriorated (42.5%) or stayed the same (37.8%), with little difference between the private rented and owner occupied sectors. The high incidence of improved condition amongst those identified as problematic vacancies in 1986, but re-occupied in 1991, indicates that bringing problematic vacants back into use often involves repairs and improvement.

Table 2.8 Changing Condition 1986-1991

	Improved		No Change		Deteriorated		Total	
Tenure (origin or destination)	**No. (000s)**	**Row %**	**No. (000s)**	**Row %**	**No. (000s)**	**Row %**	**No. (000s)**	**Row %**
Occupied 1986, vacant 1991	37	19.7	71	37.8	80	42.5	188	100
Vacant 1986, occupied 1991	191	75.1	6	2.4	57	22.5	253	100
Vacant 1986 and 1991	24	30.2	25	31.8	30	38.0	79	100
Occupied control group	1,633	53.7	747	24.6	660	21.7	3,040	100
Owner occupied	*1,247*	*53.1*	*624*	*26.6*	*476*	*20.3*	*2,347*	*100*
Private rented	*386*	*55.7*	*123*	*17.8*	*184*	*26.5*	*693*	*100*

Improvement and Modernisation

2.16 It appears that improvement and modernisation is an important part of the process of bringing problematic vacancies back into use. Whereas 37.1% of the control group of properties had been improved or modernised after 1964, those which had been vacant in 1986 and were occupied in 1991, were more likely to have been modernised after 1964 (42.3%). In contrast (Table 2.9), those which were vacant in both 1986 and 1991 were unlikely to have been modernised since 1964 (only 13.9%), whilst those occupied in 1986 but vacant in 1991 were also less likely than the occupied control group to have been modernised (31.3%).

---

[3] It is difficult to examine changing condition over time, due to the change in the fitness standard between 1986 and 1991. However, dwellings were identified as having improved, stayed the same, or deteriorated in condition:

- -major improvement -unfit to fit, high to low repair costs, missing amenities to presence if internal survey in 1991;
- -some improvement -no change in fitness but lower repair costs, evidence of improvement or modernisation;
- -no change -similar repair costs, no evidence of recent improvement or modernisation, no change in fitness;
- -deterioration -fit to unfit after allowing for effect of difference in standard, significant increase in cost of repair, increase in number of items defective.

Table 2.9 Problematic Vacants: Modernisation

	Modernised		Not Modernised		Total	
	No. (000s)	Row %	No. (000s)	Row %	No. (000s)	Row %
Occupied 1986, vacant 1991	59	31.3	129	68.7	188	100.0
Vacant 1986, occupied 1991	107	42.3	146	57.7	253	100.0
Vacant 1986 and 1991	11	13.9	68	86.1	79	100.0
Occupied Control Group[1]	1,129	37.1	1,911	62.9	3,040	100.0

Note: [1] Occupied control group is pre-1919 terraced houses and converted flats

Market Value

2.17 Vacant properties which were previously owner occupied had a lower market value than the equivalent occupied stock (Table 2.10). There was less variation amongst the private rented sector problematic vacants, where values were much closer to the average value of a similar type of dwelling in the occupied private rented sector. Those vacant in both years had the lowest average market value (£45,749).

Table 2.10 1991 Market Value of Problematic Vacants by Tenure

Origin or Destination Tenure	1991 Mean Value £
Owner Occupied Problematic Vacants	
Occupied 1986, vacant 1991	48,088
Vacant 1986, occupied 1991	59,239
Private Rented Problematic Vacants	
Occupied 1986, vacant 1991	55,478
Vacant 1986, occupied 1991	50,632
Vacant 1986 and 1991	45,749
Occupied Control Group[1]	
Owner occupied	55,113
Private rented	51,245

Note: [1] Occupied control group is of pre-1919 terraced houses and converted flats

Repair Costs for Bringing Dwellings Back into Long Term Use

2.18 Half of the dwellings which were vacant in 1991 and classed as problematic would cost over £5,000 to bring back into long term use (Table 2.11). In contrast, only a third of occupied dwellings of a similar type and age would require this level of expenditure.

Summary and Conclusions

2.19 The analysis has distinguished between two different types of vacancy:

- *transactional* vacants which are active in the market and under normal market conditions come back into use after a relatively short period and are necessary for mobility reasons;
- and *problematic* vacants, which are inactive and less likely to be re-occupied quickly unless action is taken to bring them back into use. At any one time there are likely to be about 250,000 problematic

Table 2.11 1991 Problematic Vacants: Costs for Long Term Use[1]

Cost	1991 Problematic Vacants No. (000s)	%	Occupied Control Group 1991[2] No. (000s)	%
Zero Cost	19	7.1	401	13.2
Under £1,000	43	16.5	404	13.3
£1,000-£1,999	24	8.9	359	11.8
£2,000-£4,999	47	17.5	836	27.5
£5,000-£9,999	57	21.3	611	20.1
£10,000-£19,999	49	18.2	337	11.1
£20,000+	28	10.5	92	3.0
Total	**267**	**(100.0)**	**3,040**	**(100.0)**

Notes: 1 These are the costs of all repairs plus replacements identified as needed within the next 10 years.
2 Control group is of pre-1919 terraced houses and converted flats, occupied in 1991.

vacants in the private sector, excluding those awaiting demolition or undergoing renovation.

2.20 Between 1986 and 1991, there was a high turnover within, a large movement into and out of, and an overall growth in the number of dwellings in, the private rented sector. All these factors mean that the private rented sector is more prone to vacancy than the owner occupied stock. Privately rented dwellings also accounted for a higher proportion of problematic rather than transactional vacancies. This suggests that action required to bring problematic vacancies back into use may need to be targeted towards empty dwellings which were previously in the private rented sector.

2.22 Problematic vacants were disproportionately concentrated amongst older terraced houses and converted flats. Problematic vacants were also more likely to be found in urban rather than rural areas and in the North West region and Inner London. In the North West, vacant dwellings were more likely to be in poor condition.

2.23 Problematic vacants are much more likely to be unfit than similar types of housing in the occupied stock, and dwellings which became vacant often deteriorated in condition, whereas those re-occupied after a period of vacancy had often improved. Improvement and modernisation is often an important part of the process of bringing problematic vacants back into use.

2.24 A majority of those dwellings vacant in 1991 which were classified as problematic would cost over £5,000 per property to bring them back into long term use. Although vacant dwellings generally had a lower mean market value than similar occupied dwellings, they nevertheless represent a considerable unused capital asset: the value of 1991 problematic vacants, for example, was calculated as £13 billion.

3 The Origin and Length of Vacancy

Introduction

3.1 This chapter considers the factors which explain how and why private sector housing becomes vacant, the characteristics and ownership of these vacancies, how long dwellings remained vacant and the reasons why vacancy was prolonged. Problems in bringing empty properties back into use are identified. The information is derived from a 1994 follow-up survey of vacant dwellings identified in the EHCS.

3.2 Since the focus of the research was on problematic vacancy, the survey sample was drawn up to consist of 75% problematic and 25% transactional vacants as identified in the EHCS. Of the 807 addresses visited, 77% were found to be occupied whilst 16% were vacant. The latter included property which had remained vacant since being identified as such in either the 1986 or 1991 EHCS, as well as former vacants which had been re-occupied and then fallen vacant again. In the remainder of cases (7%) it was not possible to ascertain whether the dwelling was occupied or not.

3.3 Higher levels of vacancy amongst dwellings categorised as problematic confirm the validity of the distinction between problematic and transactional vacants, derived from the EHCS analysis. The vacancy rate in 1994 was more than twice as high for problematics (21%) as for transactionals (10%). In addition, the overall vacancy rate at the time of the survey was 14% for those which were vacant in 1986 (but re-occupied by 1991), whereas 21% of those vacant in 1991 (but occupied in 1986) were still vacant by 1994, and 36% of those vacant in both 1986 and 1991 continued to be vacant.

3.4 At the first stage of fieldwork, 197 interviews were completed with current owner occupiers responsible for bringing the vacant dwelling back into use. A further 192 other current occupants (predominantly tenants) were contacted, whilst 132 addresses (16%) were vacant. From neighbour and tenant information and other means of tracing owners of vacant dwellings (such as the Land Registry), a further 68 interviews were undertaken, with current owners responsible for bringing vacant dwellings back into use (44), former owners of vacants (12), or current owners of property empty in 1994 (12). Thus, of the 265 interviews with owners, 241 were responsible for bringing previously vacant dwellings back into use, of whom 86% were owner occupiers and 14% landlords.

3.5 In Appendix B the response addresses, for which owners were traced and interviewed, are compared with all private sector vacants identified in either the 1986 or 1991 EHCS. Whilst successful interviews under-represented dwellings previously in the private rented sector, as well as vacancies amongst flats, there is no reason to believe that the pattern of vacancy processes would have been significantly different from that described below.

The Origin of Vacancies

3.6 In the majority of cases, those currently owning a dwelling which was vacant in either 1986 or 1991 were not responsible for it becoming vacant. Identification of the reasons for vacancy were mainly dependent on the knowledge of present owners of the history of their dwelling.

Vacancy generated by previous owner

3.7 Where the vacancy was generated by the previous owner, in 13% of cases the current owner did not know how the vacancy originated. However, 41% of current owners gave the reason the vacancy was generated as the death of the previous occupant (27%) or when the previous occupant moved in to hospital or institutional care (14%). A further 13% of vacancies were generated when the property was repossessed, in the case of owner occupiers, or the occupants were evicted, in the case of private tenants (the proportion of repossessions or evictions was similar for property which had been owner occupied or which had been privately rented). 16% of former occupants moved out for other reasons. These included relationship breakdown, job related moves, owners moving to live abroad and owners simply moving to live elsewhere. In 6% of cases subsequent owners suggested that the condition of the property was a factor which explained why the property became vacant. In the remainder of cases various other reasons were given for the dwelling becoming vacant.

3.8 There were no major differences in the origin of vacancy between problematic and transactional vacants, suggesting that the distinction only holds when looking at the length of vacancy and the reasons vacancy was prolonged. However, the survey does suggest that vacancies resulting from repossession or eviction tended to be over-represented amongst vacancies in London, and amongst those properties which remained vacant for more than two years. For example, whereas 13% of all previously owner occupied vacants were due to repossession, this figure rose to a quarter of problematic vacants which had been owner occupied.

3.9 In order to see if there was a difference between the way problematic vacants were generated in the owner occupied sector and the private rented sector, Table 3.1 shows the reason for vacancy according to tenure of origin (in 1986), focusing on 1991 problematic vacants only (that is, those for which previous tenure is known). Where vacant dwellings had previously been owner occupied, half had originated through the death of the former owner or a move into hospital or institutional care, a quarter were as a result of repossession, and 14% because the owner occupier moved for other reasons. These included owner occupiers being relocated by their employers, voluntarily moving to take up employment and moving to a different property to meet their housing needs.

3.10 Where problematic vacancies had been previously privately rented, unsurprisingly a higher proportion of subsequent owners did not know how the vacancy originated. However, where the origin was known, many had become vacant through the occupant dying or moving to a hospital or institution and a variety of other reasons for moving. In other instances vacancies were generated when tenants left accommodation which had been provided by their employer. In some cases where a vacancy was so generated, it remained vacant because it was not needed by a subsequent employee and the owner was unwilling to let the dwelling to a non-employee.

Table 3.1 Problematic Vacants (1991) Brought Back Into Use: Reason for First Becoming Vacant, by Previous Tenure

	Problematic Vacancies		
	Previously Owner Occupied	Previously Private Rented	Previously Vacant
Reason for Vacancy	%	%	%
Previous occupant died	32	21	15
Previous occupant moved			
to hospital/institution	18	29	8
evicted/repossessed	25	14	23
other reason	14	21	16
Property in poor condition/ Being renovated	4		
Tenants decanted so owner could sell	-	7	8
Financial problems over renovation grant	-	-	8
Difficulties in letting/Owner reluctant to let	4	7	-
Don't know	11	29	23
Base	**28**	**14**	**13**

Vacancy generated by the same owner who brought it back into use

3.11 Where the current owner of the dwelling was also responsible for the dwelling becoming vacant, the reasons for vacancy origin were different to those where the dwelling subsequently changed hands. These represented one fifth of all dwellings where owners were interviewed. There was less likely to be a change in ownership in the private rented sector than in owner occupation.

3.12 Where current owner occupiers were responsible for the original vacancy, in just over half of these cases the dwelling was occupied by tenants, friends or relatives before the vacancy was created. In other cases the owner occupier moved in, but then moved out again in order to carry out repairs and modernisation, and thus originated the vacancy identified in either 1986 or 1991.

3.13 Where the vacancy was generated by an owner occupier, half of these dwellings remained empty for up to a year, compared with 30% which were vacant for 1-2 years and 20% more than 2 years. The reasons mainly related to the poor condition of the property or that renovation was being undertaken.

3.14 Where the current landlord owned the dwelling when it became vacant, the majority of dwellings (65%) had been occupied by rent paying tenants or licensees. In other cases the dwelling had previously been occupied by employees or people living there on a rent free basis. In one case the owner themselves also lived there.

3.15 The landlord was directly responsible for the origin of the vacancy in only 18% of these cases. In a majority of cases the vacancy was created because the former tenants either died or chose to move out. Other reasons for the vacancy being generated included the dwelling being in serious disrepair or because the local council had issued a closing order on the property.

Vacancy origin of those still vacant

3.16 Interviews were also conducted with a small number of current owners of dwellings which were still vacant at the time of the 1994 fieldwork. Most of these dwellings had previously been occupied either by tenants, employees, people living there rent free or members of the owners' family. In only 25% of cases was the vacancy generated by the current owner, as opposed to the former occupants.

3.17 In summary, the most significant reasons for the origin of vacancy were the death of the previous occupant, or their move for a variety of reasons, willingly or under pressure from landlords or mortgage lenders. In particular the survey has highlighted the relatively high proportion of problematic vacancies generated in the owner occupied sector as a result of action to gain repossession of the property.

3.18 Whilst almost 80% of vacancies subsequently resulted in a change of ownership of the property, some vacancies were generated after the property was acquired by the owner responsible for its eventual re-use. In some cases, vacancy is necessary to allow for housing to be modernised. This issue is considered further in chapter four.

Vacancy Duration

3.19 Two different periods of vacancy were identified: firstly the time between the dwelling becoming empty and when it was acquired by a different owner, or was brought back into use by the same owner; secondly, the time between the empty dwelling being acquired by a different owner and it being brought back into use.

Length of Vacancy after Origin

3.20 Since most vacants were acquired by a different owner before they were brought back into use, this section concentrates on the period between the origin of the vacancy and acquisition by a different owner. Table 3.2 shows that, where owners knew the length of vacancy, this was mostly over a year in duration. Where dwellings were brought back into use by landlords, a majority were unable to say how long the dwelling had been vacant prior to acquiring the empty property. However, where landlords did know then in a third of cases the dwellings had stood empty for more than 5 years. Whilst the landlord information is based only on a small number of cases, the survey evidence suggests that dwellings brought back into use by landlords had typically experienced a longer vacancy interval prior to acquisition than was the case with vacancies brought back into use by owner occupiers.

Table 3.2 Vacants Brought Back into Use where Acquired Vacant: Length of Time Vacant before Acquisition, by Destination Tenure

Length of Vacancy Interval	Owner Occupied %	Privately Rented %
Under 6 months	17	7
6-12 months	15	7
1-2 years	19	14
2-5 years	18	-
5+ years	7	14
Don't know	25	57
Base	**174**	**14**

3.22 Since there is a high degree of movement into and out of the private rented sector which may involve vacancy (see Chapter 2), length of vacancy is examined by looking at the previous tenure of problematic vacants (1991 problematics for which previous tenure was known in 1986). Of those problematic vacants which had previously been owner occupied Table 3.3 shows that 43% were estimated to have been vacant for less then 12 months, as against 21% of those previously in the private rented sector. Similarly, only 18% of problematic vacants which had previously been owner occupied were estimated to have been vacant for over two years (and only 4% for more than 5 years) compared with 28% of those problematic vacants which had previously been privately rented. This indicates that previously privately rented housing tended to have been vacant for longer periods than dwellings previously owner occupied.

Length of Vacancy after Acquisition

3.23 In many instances there is also a period of vacancy between the acquisition of a vacant dwelling by an owner intending to bring about its re-use and the property being re-occupied. Since the reasons which explain these separate periods of vacancy are often different, their duration is considered independently. For example, 48% of owner occupiers who were responsible for bringing the dwelling back into use moved in immediately after acquisition (Table 3.4). However, if just problematic vacants brought back into use by owner occupiers are considered, then in only 36% of cases did households move in at the same time as acquisition. Few landlords let their properties immediately, so tenants typically did not move in at the time the landlord acquired the property.

Table 3.3 Problematic Vacants (1991) Brought Back Into Use: Length of Vacancy Before Acquired, by Previous Tenure (1986)

	Problematic Vacancies		
	Previously Owner Occupied	Previously Private Rented	Previously Vacant
Length of Vacancy	%	%	%
Under 6 months	14	21	31
6-12 months	29	-	-
1-2 years	14	21	15
2-5 years	14	14	15
5+ years	4	14	15
Don't know	25	26	23
Base	**28**	**14**	**13**

Table 3.4 Owners Responsible for Bringing Vacant Dwellings Back Into Use - Moved in at Same Time as Acquired

	Owner Occupiers	Landlord
	%	%
Yes	48	-
No	46	93
Don't know	5	7
Total	**100**	**100**

3.24 Table 3.5 shows vacancy duration after acquisition, for both owner occupiers and landlords responsible for bringing dwellings back into use, where the new occupants did not move in when the property was acquired. In such cases only 3% of owner occupiers moved in within four weeks of acquisition and 18% within three months. In contrast, whilst no landlords interviewed had tenants who moved in at the time they acquired the property, in 12% of cases tenants were in residence within 4 weeks and 33% were occupied within 3 months. The evidence suggests that, whilst a significant proportion of owner occupiers who are responsible for bringing vacant dwellings back into use move into their homes immediately they acquire them, where they do not it may be more than six months before they take up residence.

Table 3.5: Length of Vacancy Between Acquisition/Moving In: All Vacant Between Owner Occupier Acquiring and Moving In or Landlord Acquiring and Tenants Moving In

Length of vacancy	Owner Occupier %	Landlord %
Under 2 weeks	1	6
2-4 weeks	2	6
1-3 months	15	21
3-6 months	17	9
6-12 months	30	21
1-2 years	13	18
2-5 years	15	9
5+ years	3	3
Don't know	3	6
Base	**98**	**33**

Prolonging Vacancies

3.25 Since a dwelling may be vacant under two different periods of ownership before being brought back into use, two sets of reasons why vacancy is prolonged can be identified There were also some properties which remained vacant at the time of the survey.

Prolonging Vacancy after Origin

3.26 In Table 3.6 the reasons for dwellings identified as problematic vacants in 1991 remaining vacant prior to acquisition are given, according to previous tenure (when the dwelling became vacant). The most significant single reason, whatever the previous tenure, related to the condition of the property (45% in the case of previously owner occupied dwellings). In some of these cases the dwelling was structurally unsafe, whilst one former owner occupied property had been subject to a compulsory purchase order. Other reasons related to problems in letting or selling the dwelling, or complications over ownership (particularly where the vacancy originated when the previous owner died).

Prolonging Vacants after Acquisition

3.27 Where previously vacant dwellings remained empty for a period following acquisition then condition was the major factor (Table 3.7). Whilst 77% of owner occupiers and 62% of landlords explained vacancy after they acquired the property in terms of repairs and renovations which had to be undertaken, almost a third of landlords and almost half of owner occupiers who eventually brought these properties back into use gave disrepair as one reason for the continued vacancy.

Table 3.6 Problematic Vacants (1991): Reason for Dwelling Remaining Vacant for More Than 3 Months, by Previous Tenure

	Problematic Vacancies		
	Previously Owner Occupied	Previously Private Rented	Previously Vacant
Reason for Prolonging Vacancy	%	%	%
Previous owner unable to sell	15	30	33
Previous owner intended to return	10	-	-
In poor condition	40	30	33
Being renovated	5	-	-
Dispute over legal ownership	10	10	17
Difficulties in letting	5	-	-
Waiting for value to rise	-	10	-
Other	10	10	-
Don't know	15	10	50
Base	**20**	**10**	**6**

Table 3.7: Reason for Vacancy Between Acquisition/Moving: All Vacant Between Owner Occupier Acquiring and Moving In or Landlord Acquiring and Tenants Moving In

	Owner Occupier	Landlord
Reason for Vacancy	%	%
Respondent Not Ready to Move In	5	-
Still Selling Previous Home	3	-
Living in Different Area	1	-
Property Damaged (Fire, flood etc.)	4	-
Property in Serious Disrepair	49	31
Property Being Renovated	77	62
Other	8	8
Don't Know	4	8
Base	**75**	**13**

Dwellings still Vacant

3.28 Despite using information from neighbours, local authority administrative records and the Land Registry, it was only possible to trace and interview a small number of owners of dwellings which were still vacant in 1994. The majority of these twelve owners had generated the vacancy identified in 1986 or 1991, whilst the others had acquired the dwelling after it was vacant. Almost half of those owners who had purchased the property indicated that they had done so with the intention of occupying the property themselves, and a similar proportion of these owners intended to let the dwelling, most of them after improvement works had been carried out.

3.29 In some instances the vacant properties had been acquired almost by default. In one case, for example, the dwelling was accommodation over a shop, the whole of which had been purchased as a commercial investment. Although the flat was let when it was acquired, the tenants moved out shortly afterwards and the owner (a commercial property development company) had no intention of reletting the dwelling, which was in poor condition. The new owner considered that, because the flat was not in a good residential area, the type of potential tenants who would be attracted might cause problems for the tenant of the shop below.

3.30 Most of those properties still vacant remained so either because of their condition, or (to a lesser extent) the difficulties which owners experienced in letting. Current owners of still vacant dwellings who had been reluctant to carry out repairs and improvements pointed to the need for more generous grants and tax relief on repairs/improvements as factors which would encourage them to undertake renovation. Others pointed to the need for reduced local authority regulation and an upturn in the housing market.

Summary and Conclusions

3.31 The most important reasons for the origin of vacancy were the death of the previous owner, or their move into institutional care. In addition a relatively high proportion of vacancies generated in the owner occupied sector were the result of repossession, particularly amongst those which were classified as problematic vacants.

3.32 However, identifying the reasons for vacancy and its duration is not a simple task because of the different categories of vacant dwellings:

- the vacancy is generated but is not yet brought back into use;
- the vacancy is generated and brought back into use in the same ownership (20% of those brought back into use, but higher for the private rented sector);
- the vacancy originates under one owner, but is brought back into use by another (80% of those brought back into use, but lower for the private rented sector);
- the vacancy originates under one owner, but is acquired by another owner who has no intention of re-using it for residential purposes (possible demolition and redevelopment, or change of use).

3.33 Therefore there could be two periods of vacancy:

- in all problematic vacants, vacancy is prolonged after it is generated;
- in many cases, the dwelling is acquired by another owner and remains vacant for a period of time.

3.34 On the one hand, change in ownership would be expected to be associated with vacancy in the *owner occupied* sector, when the previous occupant leaves and before the dwelling is brought back into use by a new owner. Sale is the norm (88% of cases in the survey). In the few cases where vacancy is prolonged under the same ownership, this may be related to the circumstances of the owner, for example, away in hospital or in institutional care for a prolonged period, or to the property, for instance, being renovated, and the owner returns.

3.35 On the other hand, in the *private rented* sector, an ownership change would not be expected where the vacancy originated through the tenant leaving. In normal circumstances (58% in the survey) therefore the property is eventually re-let. Turnover of tenants in the private rented sector tends to be high. However, in a significant number of cases, prolonged vacancy in this sector is associated with a change in ownership and sometimes a change in tenure (reflected in the high flow of dwellings into and out of private renting identified in chapter 2).

3.36 An owner who generated the vacancy may eventually sell but may take a long time in making the decision, or in trying to sell:

- owner occupiers may already have moved elsewhere, or a sole owner occupier may have died and no decision yet been made by the beneficiaries whether to sell or let or there may be complications over legal ownership;

- landlords may decide to sell rather than re-let, either because of the difficulties of re-letting (often related to the poor condition of the property) or of finding acceptable tenants;

- serious disrepair (in one instance a local authority closing order) and lack of funds to rectify this led to a decision to sell;

- in some instances vacancy is prolonged because of a decision to sell, where for example one tenant moves out of a flat within a dwelling or block and the landlord decides to keep the flat empty with a view to gaining full vacant possession before selling after all other occupants have moved out;

- in other instances owners may experience delays in selling or renting out their properties because of low demand. In some instances owners may simply with-hold property from the market, speculating on an upward movement in house prices.

3.37 Following acquisition there may be problems in bringing an empty property back into use:

- the main reason for a property remaining vacant after acquisition by a new owner was disrepair and the time and resources needed to complete repairs and improvements. Many owners gave a lack of funds preventing the work required being done as the major reason that the vacancy was prolonged. Landlords, in particular, mentioned funding difficulties, and that they did not receive grants from local authorities either because, as corporate landlords, they were not eligible under current conditions, or that local authorities had no funding for discretionary grants. Others suggested tax relief on repairs and improvements to encourage landlords to undertake renovation;

- some dwellings were acquired with no intention of residential use, or as part of a broader property package. In other cases the property was purchased where residential letting was not the prime reason for acquisition, for example flats over commercial premises. Owners may not have considered letting the property, except to employees;

3.38 In some cases, dwellings remained vacant because of the perceived burdens and disadvantages of being a landlord. This suggests more needs to be done to highlight the benefits of renting on assured or assured shorthold tenancies or leasing property to appropriate social landlords.

4 Bringing Empty Dwellings Back into Use

Introduction

4.1 Whilst some properties may be lost from the housing stock, because they are demolished or change to non-residential use (4% of dwellings identified in the survey), in most cases empty housing will eventually be re-occupied, and this usually involves a change in ownership. This chapter looks at the survey evidence of who brings vacants back into use, and how and why they are brought back into use. Chapter two suggested that for about three quarters of problematic vacants, the ending of vacancy was associated with an improvement in condition and this chapter examines the relationship between bringing a vacancy back into use and repair and improvement works.

Owners Responsible for Bringing Vacants Back into Use

4.2 The survey over-represented owner occupiers responsible for terminating vacancies and under-represented private landlords. For example, EHCS data (where dwellings vacant in 1986 had been brought back into use in 1991) suggests that 74% of dwellings which had come back into use had done so through owner occupation, as against 26% owned by private landlords. In the follow-up survey, landlords represented 14% of those owners who brought vacant property back into use. The reason for this under-representation of landlords in the follow up survey is the much greater difficulty encountered in identifying, tracing and interviewing this type of owner, given the fact that they were not resident at the property.

4.3 As noted in Chapter 3, in more than 80% of cases the end of the vacancy involved a change of ownership. However, owners who had generated as well as ended the vacancy were more likely to be private landlords (almost 58% of landlords, in contrast to only 11.5% of owner occupiers, had generated and ended the vacancy).

4.4 Where dwellings were identified as vacant in 1991, in many cases their previous tenure in 1986, as well as their tenure when brought back into use, is known. The paths of tenure change are shown in Table 4.1. Amongst 1991 vacants classed as transactional, 83% had not changed tenure from the generation of the vacancy to its ending. In contrast, only 63% of 1991 problematic vacants which had been occupied in 1986 were in the same tenure in 1994, compared with 28% which had changed tenure and 9% which were still vacant. The evidence suggests that bringing problematic vacancies back into use often involved not only a change of ownership but also tenure, in particular from private renting to owner occupation. However, because the traced respondents under-represent privately rented housing, it is likely that dwellings remaining in the private rented sector or moving from owner occupation into private renting were also under-represented.

Table 4.1 Change of Tenure: 1991 Vacants

Occupancy 1986	Occupancy 1994	Vacants	
		Problematic %	Transactional %
Owner occupier	Owner occupier	56	80
Private tenant	Owner occupier	23	10
Owner occupier	Private tenant	5	3
Private tenant	Private tenant	7	3
Owner occupier	Vacant	2	3
Private tenant	Vacant	7	-
Base		**57**	**30**

4.5 Of individual owners responsible for bringing vacants back into use, 41% were adult households of non-pensionable age, 40% were family households (primarily two parent family households) and only 11% were elderly person households.

4.6 Where vacant dwellings have been brought back into use by owner occupiers the household tended to be relatively young, small, economically active households (50% of these households were no more than 2 people, and 70% no more than 3, whilst 47% of owner occupier respondents were under 35, with a further 27% aged 35-44). This is partly related to the type of property which tended to be older terraced housing or converted flats, favoured by first time buyers.

4.7 Most owner occupiers were in skilled manual occupations (62%), compared with 15% who were in managerial work, and a similar proportion who were in partly skilled occupations. Only 8% of owner occupier respondents were unskilled and just 2% in professional occupations. This suggests that owner occupiers bringing vacant dwellings back into use may have had some of the manual skills necessary to undertake at least part of the required renovation work.

4.8 Almost half of landlords responsible for ending vacancies were private organisations (including agents, managing the properties on behalf of company landlords), rather than individual owners. In some instances, the dwellings had been brought back into use by property companies (or their agents) deliberately reletting them. In other instances the vacant dwelling had been acquired as part of a mixed use (for example, flat above a shop). One property in the North West, for example, had been acquired with vacant possession by a commercial retailer in 1981, had been converted into a take-away shop with self contained living accommodation above for the use of employees, but became vacant in 1991 and was not re-occupied until another employee moved in during September 1992. Re-occupation in this case was linked to re-use of the associated commercial premises.

4.9 Where dwellings were brought back into use by property companies, these were mainly organisations concerned with letting out residential property. It was those properties which continued to be vacant which were likely to have been acquired by other types of property developers with little intention of re-using them for residential purposes (see Chapter 3).

Acquiring Vacants: Processes

4.10 Table 4.2 illustrates the principal method used by those owners responsible for first bringing dwellings back into use to identify the property they acquire. In a majority of cases this was through an estate agent, although in 13% of cases the main method of identification was simply the 'for sale' advertisement outside the property. In 11% of cases, the owner responsible for bringing the dwellings back into use either knew or was related to the previous owner.

Table 4.2: Method of Identifying Vacancy for all Dwellings Brought Back into Use

Method of Identifying Vacancy	Owner Occupiers %	Landlords %
Knew previous owners	8	4
Related to previous owners	4	-
Through estate agent	52	56
Through LA/Housing association	1	4
'For sale' sign outside	13	11
Miscellaneous	19	29
Don't know/Can't remember	5	4
Base	**208**	**27**

4.11 Amongst owner occupiers the single most important reason for the acquisition of the vacant dwelling (Table 4.3) was related to the affordable price of the dwelling (20% of respondents). Other significant reasons given by newly acquiring owner occupiers included the favourable location of the dwelling (14%), the fact that the property represented good value for money to the respondent (12%), or that it provided an opportunity for renovation (11%). Amongst miscellaneous reasons given by incoming owner occupiers, was the fact that the purchase could be completed quickly (since no chain was involved), that the property was close to amenities, or that there were no other suitable properties available which the purchaser could afford.

Table 4.3 Single Most Important Reason for Acquisition of Vacant Dwellings where Brought Back into Use, by Type of Owner

Reason for Acquisition	Owner Occupiers %	Landlords %
Price was right/Within price range	20	7
Likes area/Location	14	22
Good value for money	12	4
Opportunity to renovate	11	4
Large property	8	4
Large/Attractive garden	2	-
Near to relatives	5	-
Convenient for work	2	-
Inherited	2	-
Other	19	48
Don't know	7	11
Base	**208**	**27**

4.12 Whilst affordability was the most significant single reason for acquisition, it was more important amongst owner occupiers in London and the South, compared with the North and Midlands. In the Midlands, greater emphasis was placed upon the size of the property and its location. The evidence suggests that price was a more significant factor after 1992 (the main reason given by 29% of owner occupiers who purchased between 1992 and 1994) compared with earlier periods. This may be explained by the collapse of the housing market in the early 1990s and the increasing concern to purchase a property which represented good value for money.

4.13 In the case of non-owner occupiers, the single most important reason given related to the location of the property. However, almost half these owners gave a range of other reasons for acquisition, including the fact that the dwelling offered a good opportunity for capital growth, or a guaranteed rental income which represented a satisfactory annual return on their investment.

4.14 There were relatively few differences between owners who had acquired problematic vacancies, compared with those purchasing transactional vacants. However, 12% of owners of problematic vacants pointed to the advantages of buying a property which they could renovate to their own specifications, compared with under 5% of owners bringing back into use transactional vacants. In contrast, 18% of purchasers of transactional vacants said the most important reason for buying was that the dwelling represented good value for money, compared with only 8% of purchasers of problematic vacants.

The Costs of Acquiring Vacants

4.15 Table 4.4 shows the purchase price of dwellings brought back into use by different types of owner (although it does not distinguish the year bought). The indications are that properties purchased by landlords were acquired more cheaply than those bought for owner occupation. In addition, properties which had been problematic vacants typically had lower purchase prices than transactional vacants. Of those which had been vacant for less than 6 months prior to acquisition only 13% cost under £30,000, compared with about a third of those vacant for over 6 months.

Table 4.4 Purchase Price of Dwelling where Brought Back into Use, by Type of Owner

Purchase Price	Owner Occupiers %	Landlord %
Up to £10,000	5	22
£10,001 - £20,000	12	19
£20,001 - £30,000	13	7
£30,001 - £40,000	15	4
£40,001 - £50,000	13	-
£50,001 - £60,000	8	-
£60,001 - £70,000	4	7
£70,001 - £80,000	2	-
£80,001 - £90,000	2	4
£90,001 - £100,000	1	-
Over £100,000	7	-
Don't know/refused	18	37
Base	**208**	**27**

4.16 Almost half (48%) of all vacants brought back into use by owner occupiers, which were classified as in poor condition by those owners, were purchased for £30,000 or less. In contrast, a fifth of vacants purchased in good condition cost over £70,000.

4.17 As might be expected, purchase prices varied considerably by region with high purchase prices in London (where 45% were acquired for £70,000 or more) and low prices in the North (where 46% were bought for £20,000 or less). These regional differences reflect not only local housing market conditions, but also the greater likelihood of vacant properties in the North of England being in poorer condition (see Chapter 2).

4.18 Almost three quarters of owner occupiers reported having an outstanding mortgage or loan. Only 10% of owner occupiers who borrowed money to finance the purchase of a vacant dwelling reported experiencing any difficulty in obtaining a mortgage or loan for the property, although this was higher for problematic vacants (13%) compared with transactional vacants (2%). The likelihood of experiencing difficulty in raising a mortgage or loan was also greater in the Midlands and North than in London and the South of England. In those cases where owners did experience problems in getting access to mortgage finance, the difficulties reported included finding an institution willing to lend on the property, problems of limited mortgage advances against the purchase price and negative survey reports in relation to the condition of the dwelling.

Repairs and Improvements

Work Needed

4.19 Table 4.5 shows the work which needed doing at the time the dwelling was first acquired by the owner responsible for bringing the dwelling back into use. In general, owner occupiers considered more work was needed to vacant dwellings than landlords. The main works considered necessary were kitchen refit, electrical works and internal plastering. High priority was also given to bathroom amenities, window replacement and central heating.

Table 4.5 Work Required to Vacant Dwellings at Time of Acquisition by Type of Owner Responsible for Bringing Dwelling Back into Use

Repair/Improvement	Owner Occupiers %	Landlords %
Roof repairs	35	24
Walls, chimneys, foundations	35	30
Repointing	37	30
Window replacement	46	36
Damp proof course	38	30
Internal plastering	51	42
New floors	33	21
Electrical works	54	58
Refitting kitchen	59	58
Refitting bathroom	46	55
Central heating	46	33
Conversion/Internal re-arrangement	25	18
Other	13	15
None of these	13	15
Don't know	6	-
Base	**208**	**33**

4.20 Higher levels of repair and improvement were needed to problematic vacants, compared with transactionals. For example, 51% of owners of problematic vacants indicated that central heating needed installing, compared with 35% of transactional vacants, and 30% of owners who had brought problematic vacants back into use considered they needed conversion or internal re-arrangement, compared with only 12% of transactional vacants.

Repair and Improvements Undertaken

4.21 Given the significant number of owners who did not move in or let the property immediately on acquisition and the high proportion of these who kept the property empty because it was being renovated, it seems likely that a high proportion of these properties were repaired/improved during the period they were vacant.

4.22 Table 4.6 illustrates the work undertaken by those owners who have brought dwellings back into use. Owner occupiers had generally carried out more extensive repairs to vacants than landlords, although exceptions were electrical rewiring and refitting kitchen or bathroom facilities.

Table 4.6 Work Carried Out (or Being Undertaken) by Type of Owner Responsible for Bringing Dwelling Back into Use

Repair/Improvement	Owner Occupiers %	Landlords %
Roof repairs	28	21
Walls, chimneys, foundations	32	27
Repointing	27	27
Window replacement	41	33
Damp proof course	31	27
Internal plastering	47	39
New floors	28	24
Electrical works	46	55
Refitting kitchen	46	58
Refitting bathroom	40	48
Central heating	37	27
Conversion/Internal re-arrangement	24	18
Other	13	12
None of these	18	15
Don't know	7	3
Base	**208**	**33**

4.23 More work was carried out on previously problematic vacants. For example, structural repairs to walls, chimneys or foundations had been undertaken on 37% of problematic vacants, compared with only 15% of transactional vacancies, and 35% of problematic vacants had benefited from the installation of a damp proof course, compared with 17% of transactional vacants.

4.24 In terms of expenditure on repairs and improvements (Table 4.7), only 9% of owners who brought dwellings back into use had spent under £1,000. Over 50% of those owners first bringing dwellings back into use reported spending between £1,000 and £10,000 on renovating former vacant dwellings. However, landlords tended to spend less than owner occupiers. This supports the evidence in Table 4.6 which shows the greater extent of renovation undertaken by owner occupiers.

4.25 In addition, where owners had undertaken repairs and improvements (or were doing so), expenditure was higher on problematic, rather than transactional vacants. Over a third of problematic vacants had more than £10,000 spent on repairs (16% more than £20,000), compared with 24% of transactional vacants (14% more than £20,000).

4.26 Of all owners responsible for bringing dwellings back into use, only 22% applied to their local authority for grant aid to carry out repairs and improvements, with a higher proportion of owner occupiers (25%) applying for assistance than landlords (7%). Just over half of those who applied for a grant to undertake these works were successful in obtaining local authority support. Entitlement to grant is related to the fitness of the property and the owner's resources. In terms of value, 37% received a grant of up to £5,000 and 41% received a grant of between £5,000 and £10,000, whilst a small number of owners obtained higher grant aid.

Table 4.7 Cost of Work Carried Out (or Being Undertaken) by Type of Owner Responsible for Bringing Dwelling Back into Use

	Owner Occupiers %	Landlords %
Under £500	5	4
£500 - £999	4	4
£1,000 - £4,999	26	44
£5,000 - £9,999	24	11
£10,000 - £14,999	10	4
£15,000 - £19,999	6	11
£20,000 and over	17	7
Don't know	8	15
Base	**157**	**27**

4.27 Other sources of finance were loans. Of those owners who had undertaken renovation (or were currently doing so), 17% had obtained a loan in order to assist with meeting the costs of repair and improvement, primarily either from a bank or building society or (in a few cases) from family or friends. In 42% of cases the value of the loan was below £5,000, whilst in 26% of cases it was between £5,000 and £10,000.

4.28 In two cases, private organisations were responsible for bringing dwellings back into use using different types of grant. In one case the property was owned by a small housing co-operative and refurbished whilst vacant by Co-operative Development Services (CDS), a housing association specialising in bringing empty dwellings back into use using short-life grant (formerly mini-HAG) allocated by the Housing Corporation. In the other instance, the property had been in the ownership of a retail co-op since the 1930s, and vacant from June 1986 (when the previous tenants moved out) until September 1991 when it was let to new tenants. The property could not be relet sooner because of its extremely poor condition and a lack of funds. Eventually a grant of £1,800 was provided by English Heritage towards the cost, although this represented only about 10% of the costs of repairs and improvements eventually undertaken.

4.29 However, some dwellings remained vacant at the time of the survey because they were in too poor a condition to let and too expensive to repair or renovate. Some landlords in particular wanted more generous grant provision from the local authority, others (corporate landlords) wanted the means test on grant removed so that they would be eligible, and others wanted tax relief on repairs and improvements.

Summary and Conclusions

4.30 Vacancy may be ended by owner occupiers or tenants moving in, a change of use, or demolition. In the majority of cases in the survey, empty dwellings are only brought back into use after a change of ownership, and in some instances tenure.

4.31 Amongst owner occupiers, the predominant profile of those responsible for bringing vacant housing back into use is of small, adult households at a relatively early stage in their housing careers. This reflects the fact that problematic vacancies were disproportionately concentrated in older terraced housing with below average values, a part of the market traditionally favoured by young, first time buyers. However, nearly two thirds of owner occupiers were in skilled manual occupations, and some may have had the skills necessary to undertake at least part of the renovation work required.

4.32 Non-owner occupiers who acquired vacant property included individual landlords and organisations, such as residential property companies, developers and a housing co-operative.

4.33 The factors most often cited by owners for acquisition of their particular property included the price of the dwelling (that it was affordable and provided value for money), its location, or that it offered an opportunity for renovation. One in eight of those acquiring problematic vacancies saw housing in need of renovation as an opportunity.

4.34 The prices paid for vacant dwellings were in general relatively low, compared to the value of similar occupied stock, particularly amongst properties acquired by landlords. This reflects the amount of work often required to bring the dwelling up to a reasonable standard. Problematic vacants had lower purchase prices than transactional vacants. This may reflect both the declining condition of vacant dwellings as the vacancy is prolonged, as well as the action of vendors in reducing the price they are willing to accept for their properties.

4.35 Despite a change of ownership, in many cases vacancy continued beyond acquisition, often with new owners carrying out renovation work. Problematic vacancies, because of their state of disrepair or lack of amenities, may require major renovation. This fact, and the time taken to organise, fund and undertake such work, may delay re-occupation considerably.

4.36 Even when vacant dwellings are brought back into use, this may not be the end of the story. Vacancy is a dynamic process and the cycle may be repeated, with a vacancy once more being generated in the same dwelling. Some types of housing, for example, older terraced housing and converted flats previously in the private rented sector, are more prone to vacancy than others. In a small number of cases, properties identified in the survey as having been brought back into use had become vacant once more, and those remaining in poor condition were more likely to become vacant again.

5 Local Authority Action

Introduction

5.1 DoE guidance on Housing Strategies (1995) to local authorities encourages them to develop empty property strategies, and a consultation paper (DOE, 1994) suggests that local authorities, as part of their enabling role, should consider steps needed to expand opportunities in the private rented sector by bringing empty property back into use. Despite a growing concern with the issue of private sector vacant dwellings, and a recognition that local authorities have a key role to play in developing local strategies towards empty housing, only a relatively small proportion of councils had developed a specific policy or strategy at the time of the research. The Empty Homes Agency reported that 23 authorities had empty property strategies in 1994, whilst a further 20 had pledged action (*Inside Housing*, 1994).

5.2 A range of policy measures is available to local authorities who may use them in different combinations, according to their perceptions of local circumstances. In some cases, the emphasis has been upon incentive based approaches, whilst other authorities have made greater use of enforcement powers. Local responses to vacancy vary according to the nature of ownership, the reason vacancy is prolonged, the attitude of individual owners, the condition of the dwelling, local market conditions and the availability of resources.

5.3 The Empty Homes Agency was established in 1992 to work with local authorities and owners of vacant properties to encourage the re-use of private sector vacancies, to advise owners on ways of bringing back into use and to publicise successful schemes. A good practice guide, produced in collaboration with the Association of District Councils (ADC/Empty Homes Agency, 1994) identifies ground rules for success in tackling empty homes at the local level. These include a commitment from individual local authorities (at both officer and member level) to develop a strategy towards empty housing, the need for links with other housing organisations and agencies, the owners of vacant dwellings, and local communities, and a requirement for the strategy to be supported by resources, publicity and the necessary time for implementation. The good practice guide identified the key actions which needed to be taken by local authority departments and elected members.

5.4 The case studies detailed in this chapter were selected to minimise duplication of those covered by the Empty Homes Agency good practice guide. Six local authority case studies were undertaken to examine local strategies and practice. These were selected on the basis of evidence of local strategies towards private sector vacancies and of specific initiatives to encourage the re-use of such properties (details are in Appendix A). The selected case studies reflect a range of different types of authority in different areas and with different vacancy problems. Information was supplemented by discussion with other bodies: the Association of District Councils, Association of Metropolitan Authorities, London Boroughs' Association, Association of London Authorities, the Housing Corporation, the National Federation of Housing Associations, Shelter and the Empty Homes Agency.

Monitoring Private Sector Vacancies

5.5 The opening chapter noted the problem of accurately measuring the scale of vacancies in the private sector nationally, given the lack of a single, up to date and reliable data source which is capable of reflecting the dynamic of change. Neither is there such a source of information at the local level.

5.6 As part of their annual HIP returns to DoE, local authorities provide figures on vacant dwellings under different ownership categories. Whilst numbers of local authority owned vacancies are derived from management records, there is much less certainty about the reliability of HIP data for the private sector stock. Evidence suggests that local authorities use a variety of sources, council tax records, local sample surveys and extrapolation from national surveys such as the Census, to estimate vacancies outside their own stock.

5.7 Some local authorities derive their private sector figure as a residual, subtracting their figure for public sector vacants from a total estimate. Southampton, for example, have estimated that, at any one time, they have around 6,000 privately owned vacant homes, of which almost one sixth are likely to have been empty for over two years. This official figure has been derived from the 1991 Census, which the council admits to be an over estimate. Prior to the 1991 Census figure becoming available, Southampton had recorded that the number of private sector vacants was 4,000. The City recognises the problem of accurately estimating the real level of private sector vacancy, based upon conflicting data sources. As such, it has estimated the actual number of vacancies in the private sector as being in the range from 2,500 to 5,000, depending on the information source. This apparent growth in the scale of private sector vacant dwellings in one authority illustrates the problem of relying on secondary data sources to estimate the changing scale of vacancy.

5.8 Other local authorities have used information from local private sector house condition surveys. St Edmundsbury, for example, carried out such a survey in 1991 from which it estimated that 4.9% of the private stock was vacant. Similarly, Bradford conducted its own survey in 1993, from which it estimated that 6.2% of dwellings in this sector were vacant. However, these too have only a temporary value, and cannot be used to update HIP returns on an annual basis.

5.9 Council tax records (and previously rates records) have also been used to estimate the scale of private sector vacancies at a district level. Southampton, for example, used rates records in the past to give 2,876 vacant private sector dwellings in 1988. However, on subsequent inspection it was found that many properties identified as vacant were in fact occupied, and others had been long demolished. Although there is a financial incentive for owners to declare their properties vacant under the council tax system (and there may be some mis-use of the system where the property is in fact occupied), there is no requirement for owners to notify the council when a dwelling becomes vacant, and it is likely that some types of vacants (such as those caused by the occupant dying) will not reach the list.

5.10 The case studies suggest that district wide estimates of the number of private sector vacancies need to be treated with caution. Whilst local authorities and housing associations report the total number of dwellings in their ownership which may be vacant at any one time, their greatest concern is often with those properties which have remained empty for longer than a given target time. Therefore, they should be less concerned with measuring the absolute scale of vacancy in the private sector, than with identifying and monitoring problematic private sector vacants, with tracing owners to discover their intentions towards their properties and with devising strategies which might encourage their re-use. Although various sources of information may be inadequate in providing an accurate and up-to-date measure of total vacancies, they may be valuable in identifying and monitoring particular vacancies.

Local Strategies

5.11 *Bradford* have used data from the council tax records to estimate the number of empty private homes which have been vacant for three years or more, producing a figure of 900 in 1994. The council proposed to write to each of these owners (where they were known and contactable) asking them why their property had been left empty and whether or not they had any plans to bring them back into use. At the same time, Environmental Health officers would carry out an inspection of these properties to ascertain their external condition and to assess whether they could be brought back into use at reasonable cost. However, a similar survey of the owners of private sector vacants in 1993 met with limited response. If such an approach is to be effective there is a need to follow up non respondents, publicise the opportunities for and benefits of bringing empty housing back into use, and to consider measures which could be used to discourage owners from leaving their properties vacant.

5.12 *Bradford's* approach to private sector vacant dwellings is needs based and represents a partial response to an estimated shortfall of housing. A shortage of suitable land for new residential development in the inner area is compounded by a high number of objections to planning applications for new housing schemes in what is perceived as an already over developed city.

5.13 Other local authorities are also concerned with specific types of vacancy. *Kensington and Chelsea*, for example, uses its environmental health service to identify problematic vacants (those empty for more than a year). Area teams then maintain and monitor a register of such properties, including those becoming vacant during the year, those re-occupied or where work is in progress, and those to be considered for compulsory purchase order (CPO) action. The register is built up through notifications from operational staff and referrals from other Council sources such as the Council Tax Register and the Planning Directorate's 'Buildings at Risk' Register. The Council's strategy is then to bring properties back into use by informal persuasion or, as a last resort, by compulsory purchase.

5.14 In contrast, other authorities concentrate on less problematic private sector vacancies, which might most readily provide additional units of accommodation. *Southampton,* for example, have adopted a pragmatic and flexible approach to private sector vacants. There is a general recognition that resources are limited and should be concentrated on those vacancies which require relatively little work before they are ready to let. These are often inherited properties or those vacated by an elderly person who has died or moved into residential care, rather than larger former privately rented properties previously multi-occupied, although some of them could have been relatively long term vacancies. However, it is recognised that the longer a dwelling stays empty the more it is likely to deteriorate and the more it will cost to make it fit for occupation.

5.15 *Southampton's* Empty Property Strategy (March 1992), was designed to bring vacant properties in the private sector back into use and to provide temporary housing for homeless households. The core objectives were to compile and update an information base of empty private sector properties, to target those dwellings unlikely to come back into use without positive council action, and to provide 300 additional units over 3 years for rehousing council nominees. The Strategy has been a corporate initiative with the support of different departments and elected members, and with a three year budget.

5.16 *St Edmundsbury* also considers any empty property within its strategy. The Council has received enquiries from owner occupiers who have been unable to sell. Building society repossessions are also considered, although such institutions are often not keen to commit themselves to two year (minimum) leases. In some cases it has cost less than £1,000 to bring properties back into use, but in other instances the cost was much higher. Environmental health officers have also identified vacants, in particular agricultural cottages, though some were in such serious disrepair that they would not be financially viable to renovate and may require demolition. In *St Edmundsbury*, the strategy is corporate (co-ordinated by housing services) and is underpinned by a desire to respond more effectively to housing need.

5.17 In the case of *Brighton,* the Empty Properties Initiative developed out of an earlier Private Sector Housing Forum and is linked to local housing associations and other private agencies. The aim of the initiative is to bring empty residential properties back into use and to enable their repair and improvement. The scheme also has an environmental objective, to reduce blight and enhance visual amenity. *Brighton's* Empty Properties Grants Scheme (£230,000 in 1993) has focused on houses (as opposed to flats) which are at least 10 years old and which had been empty at least six months. Properties selected for action should require works which would be eligible for assistance under the renovation grants system. The Empty Properties Officer in Brighton, in addition to providing owners of vacant properties with information on the mechanics of bringing vacants back into use (such as requirements for planning permission, grant entitlements, likely rent levels), also co-ordinates reports on vacancy, carries out selected surveys and site visits, and uses public records to trace owners and refer owners to appropriate options.

5.18 *Leicester* targets vacants in specific areas, rather than city wide, with the focus on former Housing Action Areas, Renewal Areas, and the City's own Urban Management Areas (designated completed renewal schemes). This emphasis has meant that a corporate approach has long been in place. The vacant dwellings strategy is now concentrated in Renewal Areas, where staffing resources are available and is coordinated by the Housing Department's Renewal Strategy Team. These vacants tend to be in poor condition and need high levels of grant to bring them back into use, or the use of CPO powers. As part of an area renewal programme, environmental as well as housing improvements are included, but as a consequence cost per property is high.

Policy Options

5.19 Table 5.1 summarises the different initiatives used in 1994 in the case study areas, to bring empty dwellings back into use, these are mainly aimed at the temporary use of dwellings in the private rented sector. In some instances the use of additional policy instruments was also being investigated and some authorities were combining measures. For example, Brighton were in the process of developing short-life schemes, considering the use of CPO powers and transferring private leasing schemes to HAMA funding as the leases expired. Kensington and Chelsea were trying to combine short lifing with renovation grants. Schemes designed to bring vacants back into use may be linked with supporting mechanisms such as rent deposit schemes. Policies to acquire vacant dwellings compulsorily may be linked to subsequent sales policies.

Table 5.1 Empty Private Housing Initiatives by Local Authority

	Bradford	Brighton	Kensington & Chelsea	Leicester	St. Edmundsbury	Southampton
Private Sector Leasing (PSL)	*	*	*	*	*	*
Housing Association Leasing (HAL)		*	*			*
Housing Associations as Managing Agents (HAMA)		*	*		*	*
Flats Over Shops (FOS)/ Social Housing Over Shops (SHOS)	*	*	*	*	*	*
Private sector management agreements		*			*	
Short-life Grant					*	*
Mandatory renovation grants				*	*	*
Discretionary renovation grants		*		*	*	*
Sales initiatives	*				*	
S24 powers under 1988 Local Government Act[1]	*					
Compulsory Purchase Orders (CPOs)			*	*		

Note [1] financial assistance to landlords

Leasing Schemes

5.20 Private Sector Leasing (PSL) schemes through local authorities have been employed in all the case study areas, and Housing Association Leasing schemes (HAL) have been used in *Brighton, Kensington and Chelsea* and *Southampton*. Under the schemes, either the local authority or the housing association takes a lease on a property owned by a private landlord/owner and undertakes to manage and maintain it.

5.21 Typically, properties have been leased on a medium to long term basis (usually somewhere between 3 and 10 years, although sometimes less), at agreed rents subject to review. The benefit to owners is that the local authority or housing association is effectively their tenant for a fixed period of time and then sublets the property to a household in need, whilst taking full responsibility for the management and day-to-day repairs and maintenance. Often the properties also receive capital investment to bring them up to a habitable standard, with the increased value passing to the owner on the expiry of the lease. However, changes in the capital control arrangements for local authorities have curtailed PSL, and in several authorities there was evidence of a switch from leasing schemes of both types to management schemes.

5.22 In some cases, owners may choose to let properties, not through a housing association but through a private letting agency. Alternatively, where landlords have a proven track record of satisfactory housing management they may be encouraged to let empty properties directly to selected tenants. This may mean that higher net rents will be charged, as landlords make provision for arrears, voids and re-let costs.

5.23 *Bradford* has explored leasing properties repossessed by building societies, although difficulties arose in meeting the local authority's requirements in terms of length of tenancies, rent levels and the conditions of management. Similar problems have been experienced in *St Edmundsbury*. *Southampton* too, have encouraged lenders to rent out repossessed properties, but only a small number of properties have been brought back into use in this way. The indications are that lenders in general anticipate selling their vacancies as market conditions improve, rather than leasing them for social housing.

HAMA

5.24 Under the Housing Associations as Managing Agents (HAMA) scheme, the relationship is between the tenant and the private owner. Under the management agreement, associations prepare a schedule of conditions of the property, find a tenant, draw up an assured shorthold tenancy, collect the rent, supervise any repairs and maintenance and ensure that the tenant complies with the tenancy agreement. Generally, management services under HAMA are less comprehensive than under leasing schemes, whilst the letting period is often shorter. Dwellings have been brought back into use under HAMA in *Brighton, Kensington and Chelsea, St Edmundsbury*, *Southampton,* and *Bradford.*

5.25 Leasing and management schemes have been the main mechanisms for bringing private sector dwellings back into use in *Southampton,* with the majority of properties leased or managed for a period of 5 years by Hyde Housing Association. *Bradford* were working with Brunel Housing

Association to develop the HAMA initiative. Bradford's requirement is for smaller furnished accommodation for rehousing single people in priority need. Brunel were investigating whether they could provide this type of accommodation under HAMA, although the fully furnished requirement was causing the association concern, given the costs involved.

Flats over Shops

5.26 Other specific initiatives which have involved housing associations in management have included Flats over Shops (FOS), a three year DoE funded programme supported by an allocation of £25 million aimed at vacant flats above shops and offices. The programme was a three way partnership between the local authority who bid for grants, co-ordinated the programme and nominated the tenants, the owner who provided the accommodation (and may contribute to the cost of upgrading), and a housing association who organised any necessary works, leased the flats for a minimum period of five years and managed the tenancies. The Housing Corporation had a separate programme, Social Housing over Shops (SHOS), with a budget of £2.7 million in 1994/95 to fund grants to associations.

5.27 FOS (and to a lesser extent SHOS) have been widely used (Housing Corporation, 1995). *Southampton* have targeted FOS with the larger retail chains in particular. However, the option is not without its problems. A lot of properties are either very small or have problems of access (through the retail premises, which is often unacceptable to owners/lessors). Whilst FOS/SHOS schemes often provide separate access to the residential accommodation, it may be difficult to persuade some owners of the benefits of bringing this part of the property back into use. *Kensington and Chelsea* also reported problems with a similar initiative (for which a locally based housing association had received City Challenge funding) in relation to the complexity of leasehold relationships. They also noted that owners often have unrealistically high expectations of rent levels which cannot be met through associations' affordable rents policies. Local authorities also reported owners' concerns with who will be living over their shops.

Sales

5.28 Alternative programmes may be developed to acquire vacant properties for subsequent resale. *Bradford,* for example, repurchased empty ex-council houses under general consent powers with the owners' agreement, whilst a local housing association has also been allocated funding under City Challenge to do likewise. Bradford are also working in partnership with North British Housing Association on Do-It-Yourself Shared Ownership (DIYSO) and Tenants' Incentive Scheme (TIS) programmes, where many of the properties acquired have been empty. Housing associations in general are also involved in purchase and resale programmes under DIYSO and the TIS, whilst Improvement for Sale (IFS) and Homesteading could also be used.

5.29 Some mortgage lenders have been receptive to the idea of getting repossessed properties re-occupied. In Bradford, the Council has discussed with a major building society bringing back into use over 40 empty repossessed properties. The society has expressed a willingness to sell the entire stock to the Council or a local housing association, possibly under DIYSO or TIS. Whilst there may be a role for the local authority as a broker between the building society and a local housing association, only a proportion of such properties may be in a habitable condition and ready for immediate occupation.

Grants

5.30 Linked to initiatives designed to bring properties back into use, whether for rent or for sale, is the availability of grants to facilitate repair and improvement. Local authorities may encourage and support housing associations in their bids to the Housing Corporation for funds to improve private sector voids, perhaps targeting investment into areas where there is a high incidence of empty homes (such as *Leicester*). However, rehabilitation is frequently seen as a relatively expensive option due to the often unknown costs of renewing older housing. This raises questions over value for money. At the same time the mixed funding mechanism for housing association development also presents difficulties.

5.31 In some areas the use of renovation grants was considered to be a non starter. In *Bradford,* there was a waiting list of 6,000 applications with a total estimated work value of £60-70 million, more than ten times the capital allocation in the City in 1993/94. It was felt that resources were better spent on occupied dwellings in urgent need, and that offering money to renovate empties might be an incentive for owners to generate vacancies.

5.32 In contrast, *Southampton, Leicester*, and *St. Edmundsbury* have made mandatory and discretionary renovation grants available on empty properties. Southampton spent almost 50% of their £300,000 discretionary renovation grant allocation in 1993/94 to support the Empty Property Strategy. Owners make a contribution to renovation costs according to their own resources. Southampton have argued that discretionary grants can be an effective incentive to encourage owners to bring back into use poor quality empty housing. Grants have been focused towards landlords of houses in multiple occupation.

5.33 As noted earlier, *Brighton* has also used discretionary grants to bring empty properties back into use, with Empty Properties Grants (up to £12,000) for houses (at least 10 years old and empty for six months or more), which will be made available for letting for at least 5 years. The scheme was launched in September 1993 as a two year pilot and has been funded from the proceeds of a land sale to a local housing association. Owners are expected to contribute to the cost of works (based upon the test of resources for landlords), and to sign a nominations agreement with the council. Grant availability provides a financial incentive to accept rents below market levels. Owners receiving grant have the choice of three different management arrangements: managing the property themselves, leasing to a housing association, or using an approved local letting agency.

5.34 Section 24 powers under the Local Government Act 1988 are another option. Several authorities seemed unaware of these powers, but *Bradford* had used section 24 in relation to accommodation over shops, giving grants (usually around £5,000) to landlords in return for nomination rights for 5 years. The scheme had a budget of £120,000 in 1993/94, but was not widely publicised, since word of mouth applications more than accounted for the supply. The City believes its financial commitment to private landlords enabled these owners to borrow the additional finance more easily from the private sector.

Short Life Grant

5.35 More limited grant aid is available through the Housing Corporation's short-life grant (ex mini HAG) programme. In 1994/95 there was a budget of £19.3 million to support schemes to bring empty properties back into short term use, with a further £23 million allocated in 1995/96. As with leasing schemes, there is a minimum letting period (typically 2-3 years), which may be longer depending upon the level of public investment. Lettings are to those in housing need, often nominated by the local authority. In *Southampton* and *St Edmundsbury* the local councils have both worked in partnership with Co-operative Home Services (CHS) who have used short-life grant to bring homes back into use.

Other Initiatives

5.36 In some authorities, landlords have been encouraged to let properties directly, rather than joining any of the formalised leasing or management schemes. Whilst housing association packages may offer reasonably good value for money and minimal risks, they do involve owners in certain commitments or obligations. In some instances owners may be experienced in letting housing and prepared to take the management risks themselves, but need to be encouraged to bring empty housing back into use.

5.37 *Brighton* has produced (with DoE funding) a good landlord guide which provides basic information on types of tenancy, tenant selection, management arrangements, tenancy agreements, anticipated rent levels, the operation of the housing benefit system and the grounds on which landlords can gain possession. Brighton's Empty Properties Initiative sub-group are also considering producing a model rent book for private landlords.

5.38 *Southampton* has developed, through the Housing Aid Service, an accommodation register for single people and childless couples, whereby owners (or their agents) directly manage the properties themselves. Local authority staff try to match applicants to landlords' preferences. Tenants entitled to Housing Benefit may have this paid direct to the landlord. The City has also developed a pilot Rent Deposit Guarantee Scheme as part of its Empty Property Strategy, directed towards non statutory homeless and those with tenancies under the HAMA scheme. Other local authorities (including Kettering and Colchester) have been developing similar schemes (Jenn, 1993).

Compulsory Purchase

5.39 Where informal persuasion fails and owners provide no satisfactory assurances as to future use, there is the option of acquiring property compulsorily. *Kensington and Chelsea*, for example, has sought to acquire long term vacants compulsorily, where all else has failed. It is practice, wherever possible, to sell such acquired properties on the open market, with a covenant to bring them back into use within a given period of time. In some cases, vacants have been sold for demolition and redevelopment. In *Bradford,* some properties in the inner area have been compulsorily acquired, for resale to housing associations or on the open market (with the promise of a renovation grant where the properties are unfit). However, compulsory purchase is not a fast response to vacancy. The process may take up to two years to complete and there is a high risk of abortive work.

Costs and Outcomes

5.40 In this section the outcomes of empty property strategies are examined in terms of scale of activity and financial costs. However, since comparable data were not easily available across either local authorities or policy initiatives, illustrative examples alone are discussed.

5.41 Of the six case study areas, *Southampton's* strategy was the most highly developed. In its first year it generated 248 enquiries (with a further 57 direct to Hyde Housing Association). Thirty properties were let in 1992/93 to council nominees and a further 44 were let privately. In 1993/94 the City had a target of 75 vacant dwellings brought back into use and this was exceeded (77). A similar target was set for 1994/95, and, by July, 11 were let with a further 35 in the pipeline.

5.42 In 1993-4 and 1994-5, Southampton allocated £100,000 per annum in discretionary grants. In addition, £170,000 capital funding was allocated to leasing schemes and HAMA (over two years). Average costs are shown in Table 5.2.

Table 5.2: Average Costs of Grant Aided Private Sector Leased and HAMA Schemes: Southampton

	1 bed £	2 bed £	3 bed £
Capital works (Renovation grant subsidy)	3,500	8,253	7,500
Management costs (p.w.)	11	11	11
Rent payable (p.w.)	66	64	87
Market rent (p.w.)	78	93	105
Capital value	30,000	45,000	58,000

5.43 *Leicester's* work in declared Renewal Areas has focused on approximately 300 long term vacant properties identified by local urban renewal staff and their owners traced where possible and advised of the options available. At the time of the research Leicester pursued a number of options, set out below, with vacant dwelling targets:

	Target:
• sale to owner occupiers (with renovation grant approval)	120-135
• sale to housing associations	35
• sale to private landlords (with grant)	20

- renovations by existing owner who:

  (a) occupies 25

  (b) rents 30
- brought back into use through DIYSO 5-10
- brought back into use through leasing schemes 10-15

5.44 Leicester has estimated that it might be necessary to commence CPO action in relation to up to half of its long term vacants. It expected two thirds of owners to respond to such action and follow one of the above options. In the remaining cases (up to 50), the intention was that council acquisition would be followed by sale to a housing association (in perhaps 70% of cases), or to individual home owners, under either Homesteading or Improvement for Sale.

5.45 *St Edmundsbury* used short life grant (ex-mini HAG) as the main plank in its strategy. In 1992-93, 18 properties were brought into use, and in 1993-94 it completed 13 (with a capital allocation in that year of £200,000). In 1994-95, with an allocation of £150,000, the target was 21 dwellings. Average costs are shown in Table 5.3.

Table 5.3 Average Costs of Short Life Grant Schemes: St Edmundsbury

	1 bed £	2 bed £	3 bed £
Cost of lease (p.a.)	400	1,000	1,000
Capital costs	9,000	4,234	10,529
Subsidy: Housing Corp.	8,500	4,234	9,445
Local authority	500	-	1,083
Management costs (p.w.)	19.25	19.25	19.25
Rent payable (p.w.)	50.76	55.38	60.00

5.46 In *Brighton,* the emphasis has been on leasing, through 'Leaseline', with 340 properties currently being leased by local housing associations. Linked to this has been the use of empty properties grant. The council has developed a matrix, linking the value of the grant (from £2,000 - £12,000) to a rent payable and the period of the lease. Table 5.4 illustrates this in relation to a leased 3 bedroom property with an estimated market rental value of between £100 and £120 per week. The table shows three different grant level scenarios.

Table 5.4 Relationship Between Renovation Grant and Rent Levels: Brighton

Example: 3 Bedroom property
Approximate Market Value £100 - £120

(A) £2,000 GRANT		
Lease (Yrs)	**Rent Payable (£ p.w.)**	**Grant Value (£ p.w.)**
2	71.50 - 74.50	22.00
3	71.50 - 77.50	15.50
4	71.50 - 80.50	12.50
5	71.50 - 83.50	10.75

(B) £6,000 GRANT		
Lease (Yrs)	**Rent Payable (£ p.w.)**	**Grant Value (£ p.w.)**
2	na	na
3	68.10 - 74.10	47.50
4	68.10 - 77.10	38.00
5	68.10 - 80.10	32.00

(C) £12,000 GRANT		
Lease (Yrs)	**Rent Payable (£ p.w.)**	**Grant Value (£ p.w.)**
2	na	na
3	na	na
4	54.75 - 63.75	75.75
5	63.00 - 75.00	64.50

5.47 Typically, the lower the grant paid, the higher the rent payable to the owner, since the value gained from the capital grant is less. The longer the lease, the higher the rent, with a corresponding reduction in grant (where the lease is for more than 2 years). At higher grant levels, short term leases are not offered. The relationship between grant and rent is calculated to reflect the benefits of the grant to the owner over the full term of the lease. In all cases there was a management fee (£27.50 p.w.) to be paid by the private owner. As leases expire, Brighton is seeking to transfer properties to HAMA funding.

5.48 In *Bradford,* the Council has brought back into use 20 empty private homes (for up to 3 years each). In addition, in 1993/94 a capital budget of £120,000 was set aside for empty property scheme. Bradford has also used CPO powers on a small scale in the inner area. It was estimated that £250,000 would fund the purchase of about 10 properties. The Council intends to plough back capital receipts into a continuing programme.

Summary and Conclusions

5.50 There are few up to date and accurate statistics on the extent and nature of vacant private sector dwellings at the local level. If effective action is to be taken to bring vacant private housing back into use, then there must be better information about the scale and type of vacant dwellings, and the circumstances which explain vacancy.

5.51 Some sources of information do exist which can be used to identify the extent and characteristics of particular types of vacancy. Information from local house condition surveys can be used to identify vacants, whilst greater advantage could be made of council tax records. This may enable targeting of the more problematic vacants which require local authority action to bring them back into use on a temporary or more permanent basis.

5.52 In 1994 only a small number of local authorities had developed a formal strategy on empty dwellings in the private sector. In the light of wider publicity and advice, more will have done so since. Different rationales underpin local authorities' empty dwellings strategies. Some councils have focused their strategies towards particular types of empty housing, for example those in the worst condition, or in renewal areas. In these cases, the vacancy strategy has been part of a renewal strategy. Other authorities have adopted a broader approach, being concerned to maximise the number of dwellings brought back into use, to help meet local housing needs. However, where properties are in poor structural condition and housing need is not a priority, then clearance is an option.

5.53 A range of policy initiatives is available to local authorities. Some involve a change of ownership, others a change of management. In some instances, specific schemes have been coupled with the availability of grant aid, either to allow the dwelling to be used temporarily or to enable long term re-use. The majority of policy options have been 'carrots' to encourage private owners either to dispose of their properties or to bring them back into use more quickly, through for example privately renting. Where private owners have taken little or no action to bring about their re-occupation, and where all else fails, it may be necessary for local councils to consider compulsory purchase of long term vacants. However, these procedures are often slow and cumbersome.

5.54 Examples have been drawn from the different case study authorities to highlight the output of alternative schemes and their relative costs. Since privately owned dwellings remain vacant for a range of reasons, different solutions are appropriate according to the circumstances of the vacancy and its ownership. However, the plethora of schemes and funding arrangements may be contributing to a situation of undue complexity.

5.55 Case study evidence suggests that, to date, these specific policy options have directly brought back into use a relatively small number of vacant dwellings and that the work undertaken by local authorities and their partners has been resource intensive and often abortive. For example, they rely on the cooperation of the owner and other agencies involved, and where a bidding process is part of gaining resources for a particular initiative, then work is abortive if a scheme is unsuccessful.

5.56 However, in a context of continuing housing need it remains imperative that the most effective use is made of the housing stock and that a range of measures are used to encourage the re-occupation of those dwellings which individual owners have been reluctant to re-use. If this is to be more than piecemeal, then there is a clear role for local councils in co-ordinating a strategic approach.

6 Conclusions and Recommendations

Conclusions

Nature and Scale of Vacancy

6.1 Different sources indicate that the proportion of dwellings which were vacant in 1991 ranged from 3.4% to 4.6% of the housing stock, but that the vacancy rate was greater in the private than in the social rented sector.

6.2 Analysis of EHCS data has shown that, whilst the vast majority of the private sector housing stock was occupied at the time of both the 1986 and 1991 surveys, only 60% had the same residents in both years, and a third was occupied but changed residents between the two surveys. A high proportion may have been vacant at some point between the surveys, as well as those actually identified as vacant at the time of the EHCS. Mobility of residents and turnover of housing stock is higher in the private rented sector than amongst owner occupiers and is more likely to involve a period of vacancy. Thus a level of vacancy is necessary to allow the housing market to function.

6.3 Rather than examining a total number of private sector vacants, the EHCS analysis has distinguished two types of private sector vacancies. Transactional vacants are integral to an active market and might be expected to be re-occupied relatively quickly; they are necessary for mobility in the housing market. Problematic vacants are often in poor condition and vacancy is likely to be prolonged. It is problematic vacants which are of concern and may require policy action in order to bring them back into use more quickly. At any one time there are about 250,000 problematic vacants in the private sector.

6.4 Problematic vacancies are over-represented amongst the private-rented sector. They tend to be concentrated amongst pre 1919 terraced houses and converted flats and are more likely to be in poor condition compared with transactional vacants. Urban areas have more than their fair share of problematic vacants, as do the North West and Inner London.

6.5 Half of problematic vacancies would cost more than £5,000 to bring back into long term use. Renovation and modernisation play an important role in bringing problematic vacants back into use. Although problematic vacants had an average market value significantly lower than similar occupied dwellings, they had an aggregate value of over £13 billion in 1991, indicating that vacant housing also represents a financial waste.

Vacancy Processes

6.6 In a follow-up survey of owners of vacants, most had undergone a change in ownership before being brought back into use. Only one fifth of owners responsible for bringing dwellings back into use were also responsible for generating the original vacancy. Landlords, however, were more likely to be responsible for both generating and ending the vacancy, although with most landlords the vacancy was generated as a result of the actions of tenants rather than the owners. This confirms the EHCS evidence that mobility (and rate of vacancy generation) is greater in the private rented sector than amongst owner occupied housing. However, a change of occupancy in the private rented sector may not involve a change of ownership.

6.7 The main reason for vacancy generation was related to the death of the previous occupant or their movement into hospital or long term care (27% and 14% respectively, giving a total of 41%). Other reasons included repossession or eviction (13%), or the former residents simply moved out for other reasons. The reasons vacancies were generated were similar whether they were subsequently classed as problematic or transactional, but the proportion of previously owner occupied housing which had been repossessed was almost twice as high amongst problematic vacants (at 25%).

6.8 There was a wide variation in the duration of vacancy. In particular, problematic vacants and those previously privately rented typically remained empty for longer periods than other types of vacancy.

6.9 Two distinct periods of vacancy can be identified: firstly when the vacancy is generated, and, secondly, where there is a change of ownership, there is sometimes a period of vacancy after acquisition. Reasons for the vacancy being prolonged after generation were primarily concerned with the poor condition of the dwelling, or difficulties experienced in selling or letting the vacant dwelling, or complications over ownership. After acquisistion, the dwelling may not be occupied immediately and this was overwhelmingly related to repairs and renovations which had to be undertaken. A lack of resources for improvement was often a major barrier to the speedy re-use of empty housing. However, in other cases prolonged vacancy is a prelude to the loss of the dwelling from the housing stock, through change of use or demolition.

Bringing Vacants Back into Use

6.10 Where vacant dwellings have been brought back into use by owner occupiers, they are predominantly small adult households which are economically active, and at a relatively early stage in their housing career. Because of their relatively low market value and concentration in the older housing stock, vacant dwellings provide opportunities for such households to enter owner occupation. Nearly two thirds of such households were in skilled manual occupations, some with the relevant skills to renovate property which was in poor condition.

6.11 Organisations acquiring vacant dwellings are diverse. Some have acquired dwellings with the primary intention of letting them to tenants, others have acquired vacant residential property as part of a commercial package and may let the property to tenants, or use the accommodation to house employees. However, in some instances the acquisition of vacant residential space has been by default, with the owners having no real interest in either occupying or letting the premises.

6.12 The factors determining acquisition for residential use included the location of the property, the opportunity to renovate, and most significantly, that the price was affordable and represented good value. Prices paid for vacant dwellings were generally low, particularly amongst those classified as problematic and those acquired by private landlords. The relatively low price of vacancies may reflect their original condition (and subsequent deterioration during vacancy), and the willingness of vendors to reduce the selling price the longer a property remains vacant. Whilst the low price of problematic vacancies may enable those on relatively low incomes to become owner occupiers, perhaps for the first time, the condition of the property may delay re-occupation whilst the necessary renovations are financed and carried out.

Local Authority Action

6.13 The local authority case studies confirmed that there are limited accurate sources of data on the scale of vacants at the local level, and that current methods of estimating private sector vacants vary between local authorities. A consistent source is needed. With appropriate staffing resources, a local register of problematic vacancies might be developed. These properties could be monitored, the owners traced and action taken to encourage either their re-use or their acquisition for clearance.

6.14 Empty property strategies may be driven by different motives, for example meeting housing need, or tackling problems of urban renewal, or perhaps a combination. They use a variety of policy initiatives, many of which are aimed at the private rented sector. It may be more appropriate to target leasing and management schemes towards the owners of empty dwellings which are self-contained and in reasonably good condition, if the priority is to maximise the number of additional units brought back into use for those in housing need. Alternatively, grant aided initiatives, perhaps linked to leasing or management schemes, may be more urgent if the priority is to bring back into use some of the empty dwellings in the most serious disrepair.

6.15 The evidence from the case studies suggests that, in terms of numbers of dwellings, policy initiatives have collectively had only a limited impact upon vacancies, and action is highly resource intensive. However, even on a relatively small scale, they contribute to the re-use of previously empty housing. They make an impact at the local level, and may also have a knock on effect, in encouraging other owners to return empty dwellings into use more quickly than they otherwise might.

Policy Issues and Recommendations

6.16 Vacancy should not only be seen as a waste of a valuable asset and a lost housing opportunity. Vacancy in the private sector also allows the housing system to function, by facilitating mobility and renovation. However, some vacants do present a problem. Local authorities need to develop efficient systems and procedures for monitoring empty private housing, particularly problematic vacants. Only by developing mechanisms to collect information on which properties are vacant, how long they have been vacant, and why they remain vacant, will it be possible to target the most problematic vacancies and devise appropriate schemes to ensure their re-use.

6.17 Local authorities should consider tracing the owners of problematic vacants to discover the owners' intentions in relation to the property and establishing and maintaining a register of such long term vacant housing, including information on ownership, reason for vacancy and any action pending. Different solutions are appropriate according to the circumstances of vacancy and its ownership.

6.18 Since mortgage repossessions have made a significant contribution to the origin of long term vacancies in the owner occupied sector, initiatives should be considered with financial organisations, either to prevent these vacancies being generated, or to encourage their temporary re-use, or their sale to housing associations.

6.19 Up to date guidance is needed on measures available to local authorities to tackle private sector empty housing, and in what circumstances individual measures, or a combination, should be used, since there are a number of different options available and different funding sources.

6.20 Local authority empty property strategies should not only enumerate policy measures to be used, but should place emphasis on educating the owners of vacant properties, as well as the local community, on the benefits of re-using empty housing. In publicising local strategies, local authorities should highlight both the problems of long term vacancy (deteriorating condition, neighbourhood blight, fall in value of property), and the advantages to the owner in getting a return on their investment (for example through private renting), and to the community in helping to meet local housing needs.

6.21 Government should consider supporting, via the Housing Corporation, a targeted programme of housing association rehabilitation which focuses on CPO properties and the negotiated acquisition of private sector vacancies which have been empty for a long period of time.

6.22 Consideration should be given to introducing tax incentives and other measures to encourage landlords to undertake repairs and improvements.

6.23 Some of the most problematic vacancies are those where an owner is deliberately with-holding the property from the market. Whilst the threat of CPO action may sometimes stimulate action, in other cases the council may need to acquire compulsorily, either to improve, clear or sell-on to a new owner who has the will and resources to bring empty housing back into use. At the moment, considerable delays operate in processing CPOs to ensure empty housing is brought back into use where other options have failed.

6.24 Government should consider the scope for penalising the owners of particularly problematic long term vacancies where there is little intention of bringing back into use. Local authorities should be encouraged, where necessary, to use the full range of existing legal powers at their disposal under housing and environmental health legislation to encourage the most intransigent owners to bring empty dwellings back into use.

Bibliography

Association of District Councils/Empty Homes Agency (1994), **Wasted Homes: Putting Them Back into Use**, London, ADC.

Bone, M and Mason, V (1980), **Empty Housing in England**, London, HMSO.

Department of Environment (1994a), **Access to Local Authority and Housing Association Tenancies: a consultation paper**, London, DoE.

Department of Environment (1994b), **Task Force on Government Departments' Empty Homes**, London, DoE.

Department of Environment (1995), **Housing Strategies,** London, DoE.

Finch, H, Lovell, A and Ward, K (1989), **Empty Dwellings: A study of vacant private sector dwellings in five local authority areas,** London, HMSO.

Housing Corporation (1995) **Social Housing over Shops**, London, The Housing Corporation.

Inside Housing (1994), Empty Campaigns, Inside Communications, 15th July, p.5.

Institute of Housing (1985), **The Key to Empty Housing**, London, Institute of Housing.

Jenn, M (1993), **Rent Guarantee Scheme Handbook: Housing Homeless People in the Private Rented Sector**, Manchester, Churches National Housing Coalition.

Joseph Rowntree Foundation (1994), **Filling England's Empty Homes**, York, JRF, housing Research findings 111.

Merrett, S and Smith, R (1986), Stock and flow in the analysis of vacant residential property, **Town Planning Review**, 57:1, pp 51-67.

Prosser, G. (1992) **Empty Properties...One Solution to Homelessness?** Bristol, Shelter Regional Office.

SHAC (c 1975), **Empty Property Report**, London, SHAC.

Shelter (Scotland) Rural Housing Initiative (1985), **Who Needs Empty Housing?**, Edinburgh, Shelter.

Smith, R and Merrett, S (1984), Returnable Empties: The Problems of Vacant Housing, **Housing Review**, 33:4, pp 123-126.

Smith, R and Merrett, S (1987), Empty dwellings: the use of rating records in identifying and monitoring vacant private housing in Britain, **Environment and Planning A**, 19, pp 783-791.

Williams, R (1987), **Voidwatch: Taking Action on Empty Homes: A Guide for Local Residents**, London, Shelter.

Appendix A: Research Methods

Survey of Owners of Vacant Dwellings

A.1 From the outset it was recognised that tracing owners would be a difficult process. The starting point was the address of the dwelling identified as vacant in either 1986 or 1991. These addresses may be grouped as follows:

- vacant in both 1986 and 1991 68
- vacant in 1986, occupied 1991 390
- vacant in 1991, occupied 1986 265
- vacant in 1991, not in 1986 cohort 289

Analysis of EHCS data distinguished two categories of vacants: 'transactional' vacants considered active in the housing market and re-occupied reasonably quickly and 'problematic' vacants which were more difficult to bring back into use and which ought to be the focus of both research and policy action. It was decided to test the appropriateness of this typology by surveying all of the 'problematic' vacants within the 1,012 sample addresses, together with 50% of the 'transactional' vacants (randomly selected by MORI), giving a sample of 807 addresses distributed throughout England. 200 transactional vacancies were included in the survey sample, together with all 607 problematic vacancies, giving a total of 807 addresses.

A.2 The sample was categorised in terms of address status at the time of the 1986 and/or 1991 EHCS:

- vacant in 1986 and 1991 68
- vacant in 1986, occupied in 1991 300
- occupied in 1986, vacant in 1991 211
- vacant in 1991, no data from 1986 228

A.3 Three different populations were identified for tracing and interview: owners of still vacant dwellings; current owners of dwellings which were previously vacant (where they were the first owners of the dwelling who brought it back into use); and the owners of the dwelling at the time it was brought back into use, who have subsequently sold the dwelling. It has also been possible in a small number of instances to interview those who were responsible for generating the vacancy. Owners responsible for bringing vacant dwellings back into use were expected to have a reasonable knowledge of why the vacancy originated and how long it had been empty before they acquired the property.

A.4 The fieldwork was coordinated in two stages. At stage 1 (June/July 1994) MORI interviewers visited all 807 addresses identified in the sample. If the addresses were occupied, interviewers attempted to interview the current occupant. If they were vacant, they attempted to interview a neighbour about the property in question. In addition, information was obtained about current owners (where not present occupiers) and previous owners for interview at stage 2 of the research. Prior to stage 1, interview schedules were piloted using addresses of private sector dwellings identified as vacant in inner city wards in Cardiff in late 1989 as part of a local house condition survey.

A.5 At stage 1 MORI completed interviews with 197 owner occupiers who were responsible for bringing the previous vacancy back into use. A further 192 current occupants were also interviewed (mainly tenants, but also some owner occupiers who were not the first owners after vacancy). Of the remaining addresses 156 provided no contact after four or more calls, in 76 cases the occupants refused whilst others were in non-residential use, had been demolished or were not found. Finally 132 of the addresses (16%) were found to be vacant, including 10 which were classified as derelict. Interviews were conducted with 127 neighbours in respect of properties found to be currently vacant.

A.6 The information gathered from current occupants (who were not those responsible for first bringing the dwelling back into use) and from neighbours was used to seek to trace owners at stage 2 of the fieldwork. From stage 1 fieldwork 'full' addresses were obtained in respect of 188 dwellings and 'partial' addresses (e.g. street, but no number) for a further 30. This information was supplemented by information gathered from local authority records in relation to vacant dwellings. Telephone inquiries to individual authorities elicited information from environmental health, planning and council tax records as to the current ownership of still vacant dwellings. Finally, in the case of 43 properties, inquiries were made to the Land Registry requesting information on the registered ownership (if any) of individual properties. In total a sample of 209 addresses was compiled for stage 2.

A.7 Those interviewed included former owner occupiers (who had been responsible for bringing the dwelling back into use), current landlords (or their agents) - including housing associations and housing co-operatives, developers and other owners of current vacants. A total of 68 successful interviews were completed at stage 2 of which 44 were current owners who were responsible for bringing the dwelling back into use (21 of whom had also generated the initially identified vacancy), 12 of whom had subsequently sold the dwelling and a further 12 who currently owned the dwelling whilst it remained vacant. In addition a small number of in depth interviews have been conducted with local authorities regarding current and former vacants.

A.8 Although 68 successful interviews at stage 2 represent only a 33% response rate, this is only in part explained by refusals and no contact. In 24% of cases the traced 'owner' was either ineligible (not being the owner at the time the vacancy was first terminated) or had no connection with the property. Further tracing would have been required before the appropriate owner could have been interviewed. In other cases the identified owner had either moved again or died or the address provided from stage 1 could not be traced.

A.9 It is not surprising that difficulties were experienced in tracing owners of previously vacant or still vacant dwellings - particularly where they were not the current owner occupier. Whilst local authority and Land Registry records were used where possible to supplement information from existing occupants and neighbours, these sources of information have serious limitations, particularly in relation to dwellings still vacant and especially where they may have been empty for a relatively long time. The methodological difficulties encountered pinpoint the need for local authorities to develop procedures for identifying and monitoring empty private housing and perhaps the need for action to develop more comprehensive records of the ownership of private housing in England. It may be difficult to take action in respect of empty housing where the ownership is not known and difficult to trace.

A.10 The results from stage 1 and stage 2 fieldwork were combined and the results analysed in order to develop a better understanding of the characteristics of vacant dwellings and their owners, the reasons why housing becomes empty and stays empty, the length of time dwellings stay empty, the reasons such properties are brought back into use and the mechanisms employed to bring about their re-use.

Local Authority Case Studies

A.11 Following advice from government regional offices and discussions with local authority associations and the Empty Homes Agency, six authorities were selected on the basis of type of authority, geographical spread, and strategy towards private sector vacancies:

i) *Brighton* - a south coast resort with a high level of private renting, a significant mobile population and a large number of houses in multiple occupation, often in poor condition.

ii) *Kensington and Chelsea* - an inner London borough with very high house prices and a relatively large private rented sector with a high incidence of poor condition housing, often scattered throughout the Borough.

iii) *St. Edmundsbury* - a rural authority in Suffolk, where house prices fell by as much as 30% between 1988 and 1992 and which have remained fairly static since, where private rented sector properties being let on the open market have achieved rents well above housing benefit levels and thus often excluded low income employed households.

iv) *Southampton* - the largest city in the south-east, outside London, which has relatively low wages, high unemployment and low house prices, in a sub region characterised by high wages, low unemployment and high housing costs.

v) *Leicester* - like Southampton, one of the non metropolitan major cities group. The Council's approach to private sector vacancies is a product of their experience and success in local area renewal policies, and illustrates how vacancy may be related to housing condition.

vi) *Bradford* - the only metropolitan authority amongst the case studies, Bradford's approach to private sector vacant dwellings has been needs based and is part of their response to an estimated shortfall of 21,000 dwellings in the city between 1991 and 2,001.

A.12 Key informants were interviewed using a semi-structured questionnaire. Although three of the case studies (Brighton, St. Edmundsbury and Southampton) have also been cited as examples of authorities developing good practice in the ADC/Empty Homes Agency report (1994), preliminary investigations confirmed that a relatively small number of local councils had declared empty homes strategies by early 1994, and in even fewer had sufficient time elapsed to be able to identify any clear outcomes. The case study research provided a longer time horizon and more in-depth analysis of what had been achieved within individual authorities than the EHA/ADC good practice report.

A.13 During the case studies, information was also collected on the relative financial costs and benefits of different options used to secure the improvement and re-use of private sector vacant dwellings using a separate pro forma. It has not been possible to collect this information comprehensively and systematically across all six, since it was not regularly compiled and updated by each local authority. However, the case studies have provided a partial picture of the extent to which different options have been employed, of average costs incurred and of out-turn rents.

Appendix B: Representativeness of Sampled and Traced Addresses

B.1 807 addresses were sampled from dwellings identified as vacant in either the 1986 or (and) the 1991 EHCS, from which 265 owners were traced and interviewed as part of the 1994 fieldwork. They were either the current owners who were responsible for first bringing the dwellings back into use (some of whom had also been responsible for generating the vacancy identified in either 1986 or 1991), or the former owners of vacant dwellings or the current owners of dwellings, which were still empty. These last two categories also included owners who had been responsible for generating the vacancy. The interviews can be categorised as follows:-

- 241 Interviews with current owners of previously vacant dwellings who had been responsible for bringing the dwelling back into use (43 of these owners were also responsible for generating the vacancy);
- 12 Interviews with former owners of previously vacant dwellings who had subsequently sold the dwelling (9 of these owners were also responsible for generating the vacancy);
- 12 Interviews with current owners of dwellings which were still vacant in 1994 (8 of these owners were also responsible for generating the vacancy).

B.2 In Tables B.1 to B.4, comparisons are drawn between vacants identified in either the 1986 or 1991 EHCS and those addresses which were sampled in 1994 and where the owner was traced and interviewed, distinguishing between problematic and transactional vacants. The comparisons are made in terms of age, type of dwelling, previous tenure

Table B.1: Age of Problematic and Transactional Vacants: A Comparison of EHCS Data and Sampled and Traced Addresses

Dwelling Age	Problematic Vacants		Transactional Vacants	
	EHCS %	Traced Sample %	EHCS %	Traced Sample %
Pre 1919	68.7	67.4	44.0	28.9
1919-1944	15.5	15.3	15.8	13.2
1945-1964	7.7	10.2	14.9	25.3
Post 1964	8.1	7.1	25.2	32.6
Base (=100%)	**521,000**	**204,000**	**436,000**	**104,000**

and change in stock condition between 1986 and 1991, in order to consider whether the sampled and traced addresses are representative of all vacancies.

B.3 Table B.1 shows that, in terms of the age profile of the sampled and traced addresses, there are considerable similarities with the results from the EHCS. This is particularly so for the problematic vacants. However, amongst transactional vacants, sampled addresses were under-represented in terms of older properties (particularly pre 1919) and over-represented in terms of more modern properties, particularly those built between 1945 and 1964.

B.4 In relation to dwelling type (Table B.2), again there are some minor differences between properties identified as vacant in the EHCS and those where owners were traced and interviewed in our 1994 survey. For both types of vacancy (problematic and transactional) terraced houses and semi detached dwellings are the two most significant property types both in the EHCS data and amongst the traced sample addresses. However, the 1994 sampled respondents' properties were over-representative of bungalows (particularly amongst transactional vacants) and under-representative of both converted and purpose-built flats (again particularly in relation to transactional vacants).

Table B.2 Type of Problematic and Transactional Vacants: A Comparison of EHCS Data and Sampled and Traced Addresses.

Dwelling Age	Problematic Vacants		Transactional Vacants	
	EHCS %	Traced Sample %	EHCS %	Traced Sample %
Terraced house	43.2	47.6	36.5	38.5
Semi-detached	19.4	21.4	21.8	21.8
Detached	10.9	10.1	9.9	9.1
Bungalow	3.8	6.6	8.9	23.0
Converted flat	15.6	9.3	12.1	1.9
Purpose built flat	7.1	5.0	10.8	5.7
Base (= 100%)	**521,000**	**204,000**	**436,000**	**104,000**

B.5 In terms of tenure, chapter two noted that private rented dwellings accounted for a higher proportion of problematic vacants (27.1%) than they did of transactional vacants (17.7%). However, as Table B.3 shows dwellings where owners were traced and interviewed over-represented properties which were previously owner occupied and under-represented those which were previously privately rented. Problematic vacants identified as empty in both 1986 and 1991 were also under-represented. This reflects the greater difficulties associated with identifying and tracing landlords who have been responsible for bringing dwellings back into use or prolonging the vacancy interval.

Table B.3 Tenure of Problematic and Transactional Vacants: A Comparison of EHCS Data and Sampled and Traced Addresses.

Tenure	Problematic Vacants		Transactional Vacants	
	EHCS %	Traced Sample %	EHCS %	Traced Sample %
Owner occupied in 1986 or 1991	57.4	68.2	77.0	89.2
Private Rented in 1986 or 1991	27.1	21.2	17.7	7.6
Local Authority in 1986, Private Vacant in 1991	0.2	-	2.1	3.3
Vacant in both years	15.2	10.6	-	-
New since 1986, vacant in 1991	-	-	3.2	-
Base (= 100%)	**521,000**	**204,000**	**436,000**	**104,000**

Table B.4 Changing Condition 1986-1991. A Comparison of EHCS Data and Sampled and Traced Addresses

Occupation	Improved		No Change		Deteriorated		Total
	EHCS %	Traced Sample %	EHCS %	Traced Sample %	EHCS %	Traced Sample %	%
Occupied 1986 Vacant 1991	19.7	17.2	37.8	65.8	42.5	17.0	100
Vacant 1986 Occupied 1991	75.1	69.4	2.4	9.1	22.5	21.5	100
Vacant 1986 and 1991	30.2	27.4	31.8	40.3	38.0	32.3	100

B.6 Finally, Table B.4 considers the extent to which 1994 response addresses reflected the changing physical condition of vacant dwellings between 1986 and 1991. Of those dwellings occupied in 1986 but vacant in 1991, 42.5% had deteriorated in condition, 37.8% showed no change and 19.7% had been improved. However, amongst the response addresses, a majority of those occupied in 1986 but vacant in 1991 (65.8%) showed no change whilst only 17.0% had deteriorated and 17.2% been improved. Within this group of dwellings, the 1994 addresses seem to represent better quality vacant properties than the EHCS longitudinal analysis suggest was the overall condition of empty dwellings. Amongst the other groups the differences are less marked, though for dwellings vacant in 1986 and occupied in 1991 a lower proportion of 1994 sample addresses showed evidence of improvement and a higher proportion no change.

Printed in the United Kingdom for HMSO.
Dd.0301405, 2/96, C6, 3400, 5673, 345720.